C000132060

And the ref was called Clough

A celebration of
Nottingham Forest's
historic 1959 FA Cup triumph

Compiled by David McVay

Reid Publishing

Reid Publishing
53 Church Gate
Loughborough
Leicestershire
LE11 1UE

www.reidpublishing.co.uk
email: reidpublishing@fsmail.net

First published 2009

ISBN 978-0-9558807-2-8

© Reid Publishing

No part of this book may be reproduced, sold or utilised in any form or transmitted in any form or by any means, electronic or mechanical, including photocopying, recording or by any information storage and retrieval system, without prior permission in writing from the Publisher

Typesetting and design by Tony Rose

Thanks to
Gillian Ford, David Stapleton, Chris Jackson and Barbara Brown
Not forgetting my own special team Debby, Tom and Jess

Printed in Great Britain by the MPG Books Group, Bodmin and King's Lynn

Contents

Preface

THE Nottingham Forest double acts roll effortlessly off the tongue. Perhaps not as famous as Morecambe and Wise or Marks and Spencer but just as familiar to the thousands of Reds fans spanning generations from the Second World War to the Gulf War and beyond.

Ardron and Capel; Storey-Moore and Newton; McKenzie and Martin; Woodock and Birtles. There can be added one more to that combination, lesser known in some circles maybe but nevertheless richly deserving of an enduring place in the legacy of City Ground success.

Enter Alcock and Walker, the chairman and manager respectively whose boardroom and dressing room leadership coincided with the club's rise to the summit of the domestic game and the most prestigious triumph of their era, the 1959 FA Cup Final victory over Luton Town.

If only Brian Clough's predecessor, Allan Brown, had been in the managerial seat, the Alcock and Brown pairing certainly would have carried an even more distinguished resonance.

In fact, Harold Alcock was a relation to one half of the famous aviators who were the first to cross the Atlantic non-stop, the flyer being part of the Manchester strain of the Lancashire Alcock dynasty.

Something in the genes probably lured Harold Alcock to Newark and the RAF at the onset of the Second World War, by which time the businessman had relocated from Bury, via Kent and the Dunlop Rubber Company, to live in Nottingham where he owned the successful Gloveen factory that specialised in a revolutionary elasticized yarn, on Grove Road, Castle Boulevard.

Around the same time that Alcock joined up, Billy Walker had been appointed Forest manager in the last full season before hostilities began and by the skin of their teeth, Forest preserved their Second Division status despite defeat on the season's finale to Norwich City, who were relegated instead of the Reds by virtue of an inferior goal average.

A decade on, with the ravages of a global war diminishing daily and a degree of normality having returned to a devastated nation, a general meeting of the Forest committee was called at the Boots Social Club on the north side of Trent Bridge, the mock Tudor building that has dominated the landscape for visitors entering the city by London Road for countless years.

Nottingham had endured the terrible floods of 1947 when the Trent burst its banks and extensively flooded The Meadows area, the same year

CHAIRMAN OF THE BOARD: Harold Alcock, Forest chairman 1957-60

as Tommy Lawton dropped a bombshell in the world of football by leaving fashionable, First Division Chelsea to sign for Notts County, humble residents of the Third Division (South).

For their part, Forest had suffered also. This was the summer of 1949 and they had just been demoted to the third tier of English football for the first time. Walker, not by any means a popular appointment initially, and his tactical acumen were suddenly under renewed pressure.

Thus the meeting at Boots Social was critical to Forest's future. Clear and defined strategies were required to be implemented by men with an unshakeable vision and belief in Nottingham Forest.

So it was that Harold Alcock stood up and made an impassioned plea to the audience. "Back me, elect me on to this committee and I will help take this club back to the top where it belongs," was the gist of his speech.

Alcock's oratory won the day and the approval of supporters who voted him on to the committee.

Born in the Edwardian era and educated at private school, Alcock was the epitome of the firm but fair employer who lived his life like he played his cricket – with a straight bat. An amateur sportsman of some repute, his family albums, meticulously kept by him and cherished now by his descendants, reveal an all-rounder who represented the county at schools football and cricket while winning trophies, among which was one piece of silverware claimed by a team of seemingly bedraggled Stockport street urchins called Fulshaw Rovers.

KIND WORDS: Anthony Alcock's letter sent from boarding school to his father thanking him for his Wembley ticket

In Nottingham, he played cricket against Harold Larwood and Bill Voce during gentleman and players games in the county but it was Forest and football that was his overriding passion.

His daughter Gillian, who has inherited her father's extensive collection of memorabilia reflecting a lifetime imbued with a love of sport, recalls happy days when he would pick up a young Bob McKinlay, newly signed from Scottish junior side Bowhill Rovers, from Midland Station and pay for his trolleybus fare back to the ground with the club trainer pedalling furiously behind on his bicycle before taking his daughter to school.

"He would have opted for the underdog," she says of that meeting in 1949 when Notts County, with iconic status already bestowed on Lawton at Meadow Lane, were the powerhouse club in Nottingham.

Whatever the circumstances, the alliance of Alcock to the board and the continued support for Walker proved a catalyst, one that reaped numerous rewards during the subsequent ten years of unprecedented progress at the City Ground.

The historic Wembley win over Luton, the first FA Cup secured by a team reduced

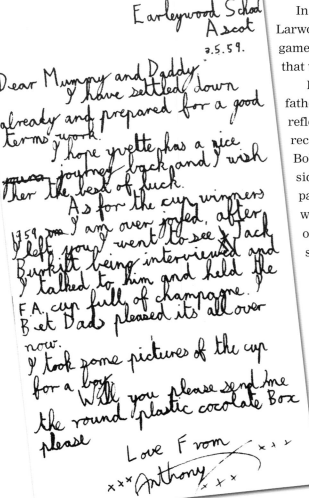

Earleywood School
Ascot
2.5.59.

Dear Mummy and Daddy,
I have settled down already and prepared for a good terms work.
I hope yvette has a nice journey back and I wish her the best of luck.
As for the cup winners 1959 I am over joyed, after I left you I went to see Jack Burkitt being interviewed and I talked to him and held the F.A. cup full of champagne. But Dad is pleased its all over now.
I took some pictures of the cup for a boy. Will you please send me the round plastic cocolate Box please

Love From
xxx Anthony x x

to 10-men, was the culmination of Walker's work, began 20 years earlier and marked the pinnacle of achievement for the club and manager, as it did for Alcock, the presiding chairman who had jumped aboard a ship that was steadily sinking ten years after Walker had been appointed.

If it proved to be a swansong for the partnership, it was a fitting one. As The Times' Football Association Correspondent revealed at the end of his match report in its edition of Monday, May 4, Alcock was part of an illustrious dynasty. "It was C W Alcock in 1873 who instituted the FA Cup competition on the lines of the Cock House match at Harrow School, went the Thunderers' theme."

Two years after Wembley, Walker was gone, ill-health forcing his departure, and Alcock had stepped down as chairman. Shortly after, the team that had laid claim to the Cup in such heroic fashion was also gone, for the most part anyway. In hindsight, an ageing side had dissipated alarmingly but inevitably with only Bob McKinlay, Johnny Quigley and Jeff Whitefoot remaining as significant players in Forest's First Division game.

As reward for his loyalty, Walker was appointed to the committee, a place he held until his death in 1964. Only five years separated his birth with that of Alcock, the latter born into the Edwardian era in 1902 that succeeded the Victorian age into which Walker first saw the light of day.

Both men carried the ethics of their generation with them; discipline and principles allied to hard work and honest toil. A letter from his son Anthony at boarding school thanking his father for the Wembley tickets that allowed him and his games master, as chaperon, is evocative of values from a bygone age, class-conscious perhaps but quintessentially quaint nonetheless.

During the last two decades of his life, Alcock retained those virtues while fulfilling his role as honorary life president of his beloved club that he had revered and revived during his years as chairman. He also served the FA Council on its Finance Committee where his accountancy background was invaluable

Yet if his reward during active service was that momentous FA Cup year, the final prize and its unforgettable prelude, there was one more bounty at the end of his Forest career.

Clough and Taylor.

In his dotage, Harold Alcock must have revelled in their success and thus Forest's remarkable rise on the domestic, European and world stage.

Before he died in 1987, he had just about seen it all in football. And witnessed the finest double-act that Forest and indeed football has ever brought together.

Introduction

IN a land long ago and far away, professional footballers plied their trade in the winter months then went out seeking another means of earning money during the summer. They cycled to work or caught the bus where they spent time talking to fans about the last game, or the next one, amid the tobacco fumes on the upper deck of the local district council's finest public transport.

Though they often cleaned their own boots and seldom could afford anything more than the average working man, theirs was perceived as a glamorous life. They were special without being precious. They were earnest, not pretentious.

Above all, they believed in old values not new money. They were working class and embraced the community in which they lived and performed. And the community responded in kind.

When Nottingham Forest embarked on their FA Cup season of 1959, their players were imbued with all those virtues and a little bit more in terms of the ability of the average professional player.

Having last won the competition 61 years previously, Forest began as 20-1 outsiders to secure the famous old trophy for only the second time in their history.

By 3pm on Saturday January 10, those odds might well have drifted to 20,000,0000-1 as the First Division side trudged in at half time of their third round tie trailing 2-0 to the amateurs of Tooting and Mitcham at their frozen Sandy Lane ground.

What happened next is the stuff of FA Cup legend, a remarkable and controversial reversal of fortunes, the agonising failure of the underdog and the start of a saga that was as compelling and enthralling as it was unpredictable and almost unbelievable.

Forest's ultimate triumph in the Wembley FA Cup Final is cemented as a historic landmark in the game of football as well as being the last time the Garibaldi Reds claimed that particular pot.

Without doubt there have been plenty of adequate compensations in the interim during the Clough-Taylor years and their legacy is likely to remain unrivalled and unique in City Ground history.

And yet the Forest vintage of 1959 also retains, demands maybe, a memory in the corner of the mind that recalls fondly and a time of relative innocence on the cusp of a decade that would change society and the world forever.

Thomson, Whare, McDonald, Whitefoot, McKinlay, Burkitt, Dwight, Quigley, Wilson, Gray and Imlach.

Not one of them a household name in their prime and probably not one of them remembered by the current crop of young fans in Nottingham or further afield.

But for a generation of supporters, on Trentside and far beyond the county's borders, their success in lifting the FA Cup that May 50 years ago evokes an achievement coursing with endeavour, dogged determination and gifted individuals who melded into one of the most exciting and popular FA Cup winners of that age.

Throughout 14 hours, including three replays, of exhilarating Cup football, physically draining for the players, mentally and emotionally so for their fans, those 11 names were indelible fixtures on manager Billy Walker's team sheet. Only once were they separated, for the dramatic last hour of the Final itself as Jack Burkitt's side stood defiant and etched their names into the sporting record books.

Forest officials didn't know where to put the Cup for safe keeping when it returned, valued by insurers at £100 to replace, four times the amount Aston Villa had to fork out when they won it in 1895 only for it to

BOYS FROM THE BLACK STUFF: Wednesbury born and bred, Billy Walker, far left, and Jack Burkitt, below, had a natural affinity but inspired in their own inimitable fashion

be stolen from a Birmingham shop window.

However, when the players returned the people of Nottingham had a place to put them. On a pedestal as they came out in their droves to pay their dues and respects. Not homage.

They were saying thanks for lifting the trophy, the city's status and their own spirits. They were expressing thanks to a few friends of the family, to someone with whom they'd shared the time of day just the other week.

To one of their own, in fact, in an era when stardust could still be sprinkled and settled on the shoulders of the bloke who sat on the next seat on the top deck of the No.43 bus.

Chapter One

The Journey Begins

Signal failure at Tooting

IT was almost over before it had barely begun. In the frozen wastelands of deepest Surrey the amateurs of Tooting and Mitcham and most of the 14,300 crowd wedged into their tiny Sandy Lane ground must have been in the equivalent of sporting nirvana as the half time whistle sounded. Tiny Tooting 2, Nottingham Forest, First Division aristocrats par excellence, 0.

This was January 10, 1959 and the third round of the FA Cup, an infamous early hurdle for England's finest, a combination of the water jump and a castle moat wherein tiddlers with a piranha's bite lurked menacingly awaiting the big fish to bellyflop.

If the FA Cup then was considered the most prestigious of all domestic prizes, it seemed that it was destined to elude Forest once more, as it had done for the previous 61 years since beating Derby County 3-1 at the Crystal Palace ground on April 16, 1898.

As the Isthmian Leaguers drank their sugar-laden half time cuppa, they were on the brink of an almighty upset to eclipse Yeovil's defeat of Sunderland in the fourth round a decade earlier.

Even an own goal by Ted 'Eddie' Murphy, whose earlier finish had secured the 2-0 cushion, that reduced arrears did not deter Tooting as Forest, universally acclaimed as the best and purest exponents of the beautiful game in England, toiled on the icebound pitch.

Enter a referee with an anagram even more unfortunate than Neil Warnock. Ron Warnke, and you couldn't make it up, awarded a penalty against the ubiquitous Murphy for hand ball, a decision just as dodgy as the rutted surface beneath his feet. The official came from Coventry but most Tooting fans wanted far more than simply to send him to that West Midlands location that has become a byword for desolate and isolated exile.

And so, with professional expertise, Billy Gray converted the spot kick and Forest survived... and how.

For the amateurs it was a cruel case of what might have been. As current Tooting president Chris Jackson, then a young schoolboy fan, recalls in his own words in this chapter the tie had captured the imagination of the

TERRORS ON PARADE: The Tooting 'Terrors' that took Forest to the brink of a shock exit at their first hurdle. For the plucky amateurs it was their eighth FA Cup venture having beaten Bournemouth and Northampton at Sandy Lane in the first and second round proper respectively

sporting public, the traditional first round David and Goliath struggle but with the Forest giants at risk of becoming the first team from the pinnacle of the domestic game to be slain by a bunch of amateurs.

Thoroughly outplayed in the first half, Forest's revival hinged on that calamitous own goal but required the sort of refereeing clanger perpetrated by Clive Thomas in his self-esteemed pomp for its completion and ultimate salvation.

"I'm not a liar, the ball hit my chest, please believe me," Murphy, in tears after the final whistle, pleaded his innocence with unrelenting conviction.

George Dring, the normally placid and sedate Tooting manager,

FRIDAY NIGHT IN MITCHAM: Alan Hubbard of the Mitcham News and Mercury sets the scene for potential giant slaying. His prediction? A 2-2 draw! Uncanny

barked the timeless chestnut "we were robbed" adding that "I would rather have lost 5-0 than have this happen."

Even Billy Gray was almost apologetic, suggesting the referee could have waved play on. Instead, he converted with a fierce and unerring shot from 12 yards. "I knew their goalkeeper was dazed," said Gray, referring to Secker's earlier collision with Tommy Wilson that had left the second choice net minder shaken and stirred. "Instead of trying to place the penalty I hit it as hard I could."

TOOTING AND MITCHAM UNITED
FOOTBALL CLUB

Member of the Football Association. Affiliated to London F.A. and Surrey F.A.

Hon. Secretary: G. A. COVINGTON, 17 St. Georges Road, Mitcham, Surrey.

OFFICIAL PROGRAMME   No. 24   THREEPENCE

Saturday, 10th January, 1959

F.A. CUP
THIRD
ROUND PROPER

TOOTING & MITCHAM UTD.
v.
NOTTINGHAM FOREST

KICK-OFF
2.15 p.m.

RANDOM NOTES

This is the biggest day of our seventy years of history and we are proud to be in a position to entertain our illustrious First Division visitors, Nottingham Forest. " Forest " have a name for clean, classic football which should be a privilege to see. Our players are looking forward to meeting the Forest players as much as United officials are ready to welcome Nottingham officials, the Midland club being the only club in the four leagues which is not a company and whose affairs are governed by a Management Committee quite similar to our set-up at Sandy Lane. We hope the hundreds of Forest supporters enjoy their visit to Mitcham. We have created two records this afternoon. We have already banked a record " gate " and this is our first appearance in the 3rd round proper of the F.A. Cup. If we win this afternoon we shall equal the record of the " Bishops " who, in 1955, reached the 4th round. No First Division side has lost to an amateur club in the F.A. Cup competition as we know it.

We are all on trial this afternoon. This is our big occasion and, as you see by the many cameras around, the eyes of the world are on us. It is important that from our captain, John Harlow, out there in the middle, to the smallest boy " rooting for Tooting " behind the goal, we let the world know what a good club we are. The combined efforts of our groundsman and Messrs. Gilliams of Purley Way have done much to make our ground, which like all others has caused concern, as presentable as possible for this match.

[Continued on back page.

THOMAS FRANCIS
(MITCHAM) LTD.
280-286 LONDON ROAD, MITCHAM
Departments :
MEN'S WEAR · TAILORING · LADIES' WEAR
FOOTWEAR · CHINA · IRONMONGERY
Established 1830   Phone: MIT 0806

FORTIOR LTD.
Platers and Hardeners
•
WILLOW LANE
MITCHAM, SURREY

BULLDOG BOTTLED BEERS
SOLD AT THE CLUB BAR
ROBERT PORTER & CO., LTD.
CRINAN STREET, N.1

Phone: MIT 1597 or 2941
BEACON GARAGE
MORRIS SALES AND SERVICE
A.A. 189/191 STREATHAM ROAD R.A.C.
MITCHAM

WELCOME TO MITCHAM: The official programme, priced 3d, at Sandy Lane wherein 14,300 fans were wedged on a bitterly cold January afternoon

This had been the latest leg in Tooting's FA Cup sojourn which had begun, ironically, with a 2-2 draw at Bromley and latterly eliminating Northampton Town, of the Fourth Division, and Bournemouth, of the Third, in the first and second round respectively.

Their eighth tie of the season had been an epic. Their ninth would be their last.

ICE COLD IN MORDEN: Many felt the game should never have started. Here's a few rutted reasons why with the teams changing ends shortly before the 2.15pm kick off

Chris Jackson, then a young schoolboy and now president of Tooting and Mitcham, recalls those two epic encounters with the Garibaldi Reds, beginning with the home game at Sandy Lane where home fans were told not to call the visitors 'Notts' Forest.

Having beaten Bournemouth & Northampton in the 1st and 2nd rounds respectively, Tooting were again drawn at home, this time to one of the best clubs in the country – Nottingham

GAME ON: A disconsolate Chic Thomson trudges back to his goal after conceding the first, scored by Albert Grainger after the goalkeeper was undone by a dreadful bounce on the wicked surface

Forest. At that time Forest were 7th in the old First Division, just two points behind Manchester United with a game in hand.

Tooting had enjoyed runs in the FA Cup before and had lost narrowly to Millwall & Queens Park Rangers in earlier seasons but had never

LONG SHOT SURPRISE: A more orthodox finish beats Thomson this time. Thirty five minutes played and Tooting have cruised into a two goal lead after Ted Murphy's shot from distance sails into the back of the net. Note the outside broadcast cameras for BBC's Sportsview in their temporary home amid improvised terracing

MURPHY'S FLAW: Just as the treacherous pitch had earlier deceived Thomson, so Ray Secker is undone by Murphy's back pass nine minutes after half time and the Tooting left half completes the unenviable feat of scoring at both ends. The Forest revival gathers momentum

previously reached the 3rd round. Although our Sandy Lane ground had been full to its 18,000 capacity before, the publicity that surrounded this game made it the greatest day in the club's 70-year history.

I had been supporting Tooting since, as a three-year-old in 1951, my father took me to a game for the first time. For most of the Fifties and indeed the early Sixties the team had been one of the finest in the non-league with many exciting matches and large crowds. In the programme prior to the Forest game the supporters were lectured as how to address the Forest team. We were instructed not to call them 'Notts' as this might

cause offence. Tooting obviously wanted to create a good impression in front of the watching country. Just before the Forest match was played my father had to go to Africa on business and I therefore made my way to the ground by bus. As the bus arrived in Mitcham I was struck by the thousands of people walking across Figges Marsh to the ground.

There was some doubt all week as to whether the game would be played at all. The Tooting officials had worked very hard on the ground and at the last minute the referee gave permission for the game to go ahead. Anybody who has seen the Pathe news film of the game will know that today the game would have been postponed.

Forest obviously were not used to playing in such a tight compact

THE REFEREE'S A WARNKE: Same goalmouth, same result as Secker is beaten by the pace of Billy Gray's penalty, awarded in the most controversial circumstances

ROUND 3:
Nottingham Forest v Tooting & Mitcham United, at Tooting on Saturday January 10
Nottingham Forest: *Thomson; Whare, McDonald; Whitefoot, McKinlay, Burkitt; Dwight, Quigley, Wilson, Gray, Imlach.* Tooting & Mitcham: *Secker; Harlow, Edwards; Holden, Bennett, Murphy; Grainger, Viney, Hasty, Slade, Flanagan.* Goal-scorers: For Forest, *Murphy (own goal) in 52 minutes, Gray (penalty) in 75 minutes.* For Tooting, *Grainger (20), Murphy (35)* Result: *Nottingham Forest 2 Tooting & Mitcham 2.* Attendance *14,300*

ground, and that and the icy conditions coupled with Tooting's enthusiasm and skill made for an uncomfortable first half for the professionals. Our centre-forward Paddy Hasty, who was to represent Great Britain in the Rome Olympics and who had just turned down an approach from Everton to turn professional, hit the Forest bar from the touchline early in a first half, which the amateurs dominated. Right-winger Albert Grainger scored the first goal after a mix-up in the Forest defence and then Ted Murphy hit an unstoppable shot from 30 yards, which gave Thompson in the Forest goal no chance. Forest, who had barely mustered a shot in the first half, looked a beaten team. Their main threat appeared to be on the wings where Stewart Imlach and Roy Dwight had to be marked tightly.

Forest, probably having been given a rocket at half time by manager Billy Walker, started to come into the game in the second half. The game

turned when an innocent back pass from Ted Murphy to our reserve goalkeeper Ray Secker skidded on the icy pitch into the net. Our regular goalkeeper Wally Pearson who had played such an important part in the previous Cup wins missed this game through injury but recovered in time to play at the City Ground in the replay. Fifteen minutes from the end came the incident that all of the Tooting fans who were present at that game will never forget.

A cross from Stewart Imlach hit Ted Murphy on the shoulder and the referee gave a penalty. Billy Gray gratefully slammed the penalty home to give Forest the draw.

On reading the national newspaper reports of the game one can only draw the conclusion that Mr Warnke

THAT HAMLET MOMENT: Captain John Harlow savours the moment with a cigar and a bottle of bubbly with the luckless Ray Secker. A great result for Tooting tinged with shades of what might have been and the knowledge that their time for giant slaying had passed

of Coventry was the only person in the ground who thought it was a penalty. Unfortunately he was the referee and so we did not become the first amateur team to beat a First Division team. I believe that after another controversial decision later in the season Mr Warnke was removed as a referee from the league list.

An incredible statistic of this match was that just one policeman present in the ground controlled the crowd of 16000 people. My father had arranged for me to be collected by a friend in his car and amazingly he parked right outside the ground. Nobody travelled by car in those days.

POST MATCH ANALYSIS: Even without the incisive comment of couch potato pundits and slow motion replays, both national and local correspondents concur that the referee got it wrong in awarding Forest *that* penalty. Still pictures from BBC's Sportsview cameras and even Billy Gray bear testament to the injustice of it all

Tooting players Ted Murphy and Brian Bennett reading the cancellation notice at St. Pancras Station to-day.

MONDAY CUP REPLAY A BLOW TO TOOTING

By VICTOR RAILTON

JOHN HARLOW, skipper of the last FA Cup amateur Tooting and Mitcham, was the most disappointed member of his team to-day when it was announced at St. Pancras station that their third round replay with Nottingham Forest was postponed until Monday.

For cigar - smoking Harlow, strong man of the Tooting defence, realised he would miss Monday's game because he starts a new job on that day, and it would be unfair to ask for time off.

Said the 28-year-old surveyor from Richmond: "How could I possibly ask my new boss to give me the first day off? I hope my club will not approach him."

While the viewpoint of Harlow, a married man with two children, can be understood, I'm certain that not even the toughest boss would prevent him playing.

Flanagan, Too

Denzil Flanagan, left-wing star of the Tooting Terrors, is also doubtful about his availability for the Monday game . . . and rushed back to his Guildford School so as not to miss too much of his teaching duty.

Before his arrival I approached Mr. E. Raynham, headmaster of the Pewley School, Guildford, who told me:

"I managed to secure permission for Denzil to get time off to-day, and since he will not miss many of his duties, I will apply for his release on Monday."

Rest of the Tooting side will be unchanged, although several have to approach their employers.

Deputy Pilgrim

Norman Pilgrim, 23-year-old reserve who deputised successfully for Harlow in the Bournemouth tie, is expected to do so again on Monday.

Last week Pilgrim, 23-year-old docker from Dulwich, was considering an offer to join Hendon but turned down the chance out of loyalty to his present side.

Referee, Mr. Ron Warnke (Coventry), who inspected the ice-covered Nottingham pitch to-day, said: "It is one of the worst I have ever seen, and a very different story from conditions at Tooting last week."

WHAT ABOUT THE WORKERS! News that the replay, postponed because of the Arctic conditions and rescheduled for the following Monday, left some Tooting players with their day jobs to consider

All aboard and back on track at the City Ground

STAGING the replay was fraught with problems because of the freezing temperatures that were gripping the country in the winter of '59. While the weather wreaked havoc with sport and the country in general, the midweek rescheduling of the match disrupted the lives of the amateurs who had the pressing matter of their day jobs to ponder and preserve. The cigar-smoking captain John Harlow, a surveyor, was starting a new job with new employers and feared he would miss the replay, whenever it might eventually be played while amateur international colleague Denzil Flanagan was concerned how his employers at Guilford School would view their teacher taking time off during midweek.

In the event, the replay took place on a Saturday, a fortnight after the original game, ensuring all the Tooting squad were available including the recalled goalkeeper Wally Pearson, the first choice who was absent

from the 2-2 draw with a double fracture of the cheekbone sustained on Boxing Day. It also allowed Chris Jackson, as he himself explains, the opportunity to see a match he thought beyond his reach while studying for 11+ examinations.

PICK THAT ONE OUT: Forest take the lead with a belter of a shot from Roy Dwight

Pearson's deputy Ray Secker had acquitted himself well in the first match and had no hope of stopping Gray's penalty but was blamed for Murphy's own goal which had rekindled Forest ambitions when there seemed no way back in the game.

Gamely though Pearson performed, his task was also a forlorn one as Tooting capitulated 3-0. A bumper 42,362 crowd, doubtless starved of football during the cold snap and eager to see the gallant non-leaguers, helped cushion the disappointment of defeat with a £4,000 bonus pay day for Tooting and Mitcham. In total, they received £5,000 from their Cup run, intended to elevate Sandy Lane's status to that of one the best non-league grounds in the country. It never did happen.

Still, the players ended up out of pocket after a thief rifled through their overcoats while they lunched at a nearby hotel before the game.

Most had some money pinched while coach Cecil Dale had a cigarette lighter and his return ticket to St Pancras stolen. Worst of all was the theft of an autograph book given to amateur international centre forward

OVER THE TOP: Another Forest attack but this time goalkeeper Wally Pearson sees it safely over the top

Paddy Hasty by a 12-year-old Tooting fan unable to get to the game. He'd asked Hasty to get the signatures of the Forest players and the book was full of famous autographs across the sporting spectrum, an irreplaceable item.

"It was a mean theft," said Hasty. Even in Robin Hood country, there was no chance of wealth or item redistribution. A fortnight after a mugging of sorts at Sandy Lane, that feeling of being robbed lingered for Tooting and Mitcham.

Chris Jackson recalls the bonhomie and generosity of Nottingham folk during the City Ground replay

I obviously stood no chance of seeing the replay. I was right in the middle of my 11+ examinations at school and it was going to be played mid-week. The snow that had caused a number of postponements up and down the country then came to my rescue and the game was eventually played two weeks after the original on a Saturday. My father, having returned from Africa, decided to go up to Nottingham by train and we travelled in the same carriage as the team. Amazingly they all looked relaxed. They were just about to play in front of 42000 people and it didn't seem to worry them.

I remember getting a taxi from the station to the ground and the driver, realising we were Tooting supporters, commented that weren't the club being a bit presumptuous talking about playing our 4th round match at Stamford Bridge if we were successful in the replay. He was right of course but I remember saying to him that we had already beaten Forest once so why couldn't we do it again.

My delight at being allowed to go to the replay was followed by my dismay at not being able to see a thing from the top of the terraces. The Forest supporters then came to my rescue. There was a high wall at the back of the ground and they lifted me on to the top of the wall where I had a perfect view. No health & safety then. I will never forget how kind these guys were.

The game was fairly predictable. Although Forest started nervously their class came to the fore and they controlled the game. There was a period in the second half when Tooting were 2-0 down when we should have scored and that would have made the game interesting. My main memory is how well the Tooting defence played, particularly our goalkeeper Wally

ROUND 3 Replay at the City Ground, Saturday January 24
Nottingham Forest: *Thomson; Whare, McDonald; Whitefoot, McKinlay, Burkitt; Dwight, Quigley, Wilson; Gray, Imlach.* Tooting & Mitcham: *Pearson; Harlow, Edwards; Holden, Bennett, Murphy; Grainger, Viney, Hasty, Slade, Flanagan.* Goal-scorers: For Forest, *Dwight (28), Wilson (36), Imlach (89).* Result: *Nottingham Forest 3 Tooting & Mitcham 0.* Attendance: *42,362*

2-0 TO THE REDS: Tommy Wilson has the beating of Pearson, the no.1 who missed the first game because of injury. His agility kept the scoreline down to a respectable three goals margin in the replay

Pearson, and what a difference it might have made if he had played in the home game. Many Tooting supporters still feel that Wally was the best keeper we ever had, better even than Alex Stepney who took his place in the Tooting team and later did quite well with a team called Manchester United. The final score of 3-0 probably flattered us.

In hindsight

At the end of the season we were so proud that the club that had ended our Cup run in January lifted the trophy at Wembley. We were actually mentioned in the Cup Final programme.

Over the next two seasons our players took the field at Stamford Bridge, Craven Cottage, Highbury and the Den in various cup competitions (London Senior and London Challenge Cups) in front of five figure crowds but never of course in front of 42,000 people.

In the Seventies, after a period in the doldrums, we employed a new manager by the name of Roy Dwight. In 1975-1976 Roy took us to the 4th round of the FA Cup and the quarter final of the FA Trophy, our most successful season in the two main national competitions. It was a very sad moment when we attended Roy's funeral a few years ago. A senior official represented Nottingham Forest which was good to see.

THE END OF A DREAM – AND ROBBED BY A HOOD! The Mitcham and Mercury News reflects on a brave defeat and the financial windfall of the Cup run although many of the Tooting players were out of pocket after a thief had rifled through their belongings in a Nottingham hotel

Tooting and Mitcham are out of the cup . . . but in the money

Note the determined look of Albert Grainger as he fires a shot past the outstretched leg of Forest centre-half Bob McKinlay. This was United's best chance, for goalkeeper Thomson could only parry out the ball. But Paddy Hasty (extreme left) sliced his shot when he moved into the centre to shoot at an open goal. Another picture on page nine.

TOOTING and Mitcham's magnificent F.A. Cup run is over. On Saturday they went down fighting in their third round replay at Nottingham Forest. But they were gallant in defeat . . . and were richly compensated by a share in a 43,236 gate and £6,200 receipts.

Cup glory has brought the club nearly £5,000. Almost £4,000 of this came in their two games with the First Division side. The money will go towards making Sandy Lane the

best amateur soccer ground in the country.

It will help to pay for the completion of the £15,000 stand and other ground improvements including a gymnasium, new clubhouse and eventually covered terracing.

Three thousand Tooting supporters, a thousand more than expected, made the trip to the Midlands on Saturday. They saw the amateurs outclassed, but not disgraced on the famous City ground.

But for the players it was not such a happy outing. They were robbed— literally.

While they were lunching at an

hotel near the ground a sneak thief rifled their overcoats. Most of the players had small sums of money stolen and coach Cecil Dale had a cigarette lighter and his return ticket to St. Pancras taken.

The player most upset about the incident, however, was Paddy Hasty. Taken from his pocket was an autograph book belonging to a 12-year-old fan in Tooting who had asked the centre forward to obtain the signatures of the Forest players, as he could not make the trip himself.

The book was crammed with the names of famous sportsmen and

entertainers. " I think it was a m... theft," said Paddy. " It's one those things that is impossible replace."

Now it's time for Tooting to their attention to the Amateur (Saturday) they must travel again either Evenwood Town in Du or Hallam in Yorkshire. Small der the club are asking: Ha cup luck changed ?

● On page nine Alan H hard reports on the Nott ham match and previ tomorrow's clash with Hen

Tooting and Mitcham United Football Club

T.&M.U.F.C.

Member Football Association
Affiliated to the Surrey F.A. and London F.A.
Member of Isthmian League

Ground :
Sandy Lane, Streatham Road,
Mitcham
Ground Phone : MITcham 3248

Colours :
Black & White Vertical Striped
Shirts, Black Knickers

Athenian League—Champions 1950, 1955
London Senior Cup—Winners 1943, 1949; Finalists 1944, 1945
Surrey Senior Cup—Winners 1938, 1944, 1945, 1953; Finalists 1940, 1949, 1956
Surrey Senior Shield—Winners, 1952
South Thames Cup—Finalists 1954

President : J. T. TRING, Esq.

Please reply to

4, Rustington Walk.

Morden, Surrey.

Chairman :
H. W. WALTERS
4 Rustington Walk, Morden
MITcham 2639

Hon. Secretary :
G. A. COVINGTON
17 St. Georges Road, Mitcham
MITcham 1456

Hon. Match Secretary :
A. STRIKE
57 Romberg Road,
Upper Tooting, S.W.17
BALham 3030
BALham 4851 (Office)

Hon. Treasurer :
F. H. SEABROOK
20 Winifred Road, Merton,
S.W.19
LIBerty 3390

Hon. Asst. Treasurer :
R. O. CRESSWELL
104, Bond Road, Mitcham
MITcham 7632

4th May 1959

Dear Mr. Alcock,

I write to thank you on behalf of my wife and myself for the wonderful evening you gave us at your Celebration Banquet. It was an evening, the memory of which I shall long cherish, made all the more memorable by the wonderful victory of your team in the face of great adversity.

It may never be our good fortune for our respective Clubs to meet again but I do hope that at some future time, we shall have the pleasure of seeing you and your delightful colleagues.

With renewed thanks and congratulations.

I remain,

Yours sincerely,

H. W. Walters

H.W.Alcock Esq.,
Chairman,
Nottingham Forest Football Club.
City Ground.
NOTTINGHAM.

REDS LETTER DAY: Gone but not forgotten, H W Walters, the Tooting and Mitcham chairman, sends a letter of personal thanks to Harold Alcock, his Forest counterpart, after attending Forest's FA Cup banquet at the Savoy in London

My daughter attended Nottingham Trent University in the mid-Nineties and on one of my visits to see her I decided to go to the City Ground. On speaking to one of the officials and explaining that some 40 years before I had attended a match there, he very kindly let me look around the ground. I was extremely impressed at the set-up and the magnificent stands and tried to work out exactly where the wall was that I sat on in 1959.

Our supporters, even to this day, when things aren't going well still chant 'we wuz robbed in '59' even though the match took place before they were born.

Last year I holidayed in Dubai and at the airport saw a book written by Stewart Imlach's son, which I found very interesting. His comments on the Tooting match were fascinating.

Every time I open my wardrobe at home I am reminded of the 1959 Forest team. At the top of the cupboard is a little brown ball with some signatures on it. Although some have faded I can still make out Stewart Imlach, Billy Gray, Jack Burkitt, John Quigley, Billy Whare, and the great Roy Dwight. A great memory of a wonderful time in my life.

Chapter 2

Delayed reactions

East coast visitors derailed

Round 4:
Nottingham Forest
v. Grimsby Town, on
Wednesday, January
28th, at City Ground
Nottingham Forest:
Thomson; Whare,
McDonald; Whitefoot,
McKinlay, Burkitt;
Dwight, Quigley,
Wilson, Gray, Imlach.
Grimsby Town:
Barnett; Batley,
Richardson;
Welbourne, Jobling,
Cockerill; Scott,
Cullen, Rafferty,
Stocking, Fell.
Goal-scorers: For
Forest, *Whitefoot (3),*
Gray (38, 44 penalty),
Wilson (60). For
Grimsby, *Scott (76).*
Result: *Nottingham*
Forest 4 Grimsby
Town 1.
Attendance:: *34, 289*

DURING an ill-advised and ill-fated spell with Grimsby Town, Jeff Whitefoot recalled that he put on weight dramatically, so much so that they named a fishing trawler in the North Sea fleet after him. At least, so the story goes direct from the horse's mouth.

Whether it was Cleethorpes' fish and chip emporiums or a training regime designed by Billy Bunter, Whitefoot amazed even himself by signing for the North Lincolnshire club and turning down Forest when, as one of the original Busby Babes, he departed Manchester United in 1957. "I don't know what possessed me, I must have been under hypnosis," he once recalled laughingly.

Two years on, the stylish right half was lean and mean and had ample opportunity to erase the memories of that self-imposed exile on the East Coast as Forest's reward for overcoming Tooting and Mitcham was a fourth round home tie with Grimsby Town.

The Mariners arrived with attitude, though, having beaten Manchester City in the previous round. Curiously they had also drawn their first game, at Blundell Park, 2-2 with the 1956 Cup holders but then caused something

TIGHT CORNER:
Billy Gray scores
direct from a corner
as Grimsby concede
another goal after
Jeff Whitefoot's
third minute volley
had opened the
scoring

of an upset with a 2-1 win as the second division stragglers defeated their first division opponents at Maine Road.

The fourth round tie was staged just four days after the Tooting replay to balance the backlog of FA Cup ties that the cold snap had created. Just over 8,000 less fans turned out on Wednesday afternoon but still 34,289 was a creditable effort by the locals and those who had made the torturous route from Grimsby.

Whitefoot had signed in the summer but had not yet registered a goal for his new club. Needless to say, how these things work in football, it took him less than three minutes to break his duck with a splendid volley against his former employers, an early defensive breach being the first of a repeat performance for the remainder of the tie really.

Two goals from Billy Gray, one of them another clinically despatched penalty, effectively ended the contest, such as it was, before half time and a trademark Tommy Wilson header, following an equally trademark dashing run and centre from Stewart Imlach secured a four goal lead on the hour before Johnny Scott's hopeful punt drifted in under Chic Thomson's crossbar. A small crumb of comfort for a thoroughly outplayed Grimsby team.

GONE FISHING: Tommy Wilson in familiar predatory action as his header from Stewart Imlach's centre adds a fourth for Forest

FINAL FLING:
With just a minute
remaining on the
clock, Tommy Wilson
nets the equaliser at
St Andrew's beyond
a despairing England
goalkeeper Gil
Merrick that earned
the Reds a replay

This was an ominous victory as well. The last time the two sides had opposed one another in the FA Cup, Forest reached the semi finals of the competition. That was in 1900. Two years previously, they had also sparred with one another, Forest again emerging triumphant. Only then, they progressed all the way and won the trophy at Crystal Palace against Derby County in 1898!

Kismet indeed...

Round 5:
Nottingham Forest v
Birmingham City on
Saturday, February
14, at Birmingham.
Nottingham Forest:
Thomson; Whare,
McDonald; Whitefoot,
McKinlay, Burkitt;
Dwight, Quigley,
Wilson, Gray, Imlach.
Birmingham City:
Merrick; Hall, Allen;
Watts, Smith, Neal;
Astall, Gordon, Orritt,
Larkin, Hooper.
Goal-scorers: For
Forest, *Wilson (89).*
For Birmingham,
Astall (30).
Result: *Nottingham*
Forest 1 Birmingham
City 1.
Attendance: *55,300*

Leaves on the line at Birmingham

THEY met at St Andrew's on St Valentine's Day. No love lost between the two rivals, of course, but by the time Forest and Birmingham City had parted company, after some close and enduring tussles, familiarity appeared to have bred a degree of contempt.

Certainly that's how it seemed during their third encounter on the neutral turf of Leicester City's Filbert Street where Forest put their second city opponents well and truly to the sword.

How different it all seemed in Birmingham on February 14th as Gordon Astall's 30th minute effort seized the initiative for the home team, a grasp they seldom looked like loosening until the very last minute of the tie when Tommy Wilson popped up at the far post. Later, the Forest goalscorer recounted his own version of that dramatic equaliser.

SAME AGAIN – UP AND UNDER AND ONWARDS: George Allen and Trevor Smith scurry back towards goal but the Birmingham defenders are beaten by Roy Dwight's lob that levelled the scores at the City Ground with only five minutes remaining of extra time

"Joe McDonald's free kick came to me beautifully but after I had hit it with my head it seemed an age before it entered the net. It was one of my greatest ever moments."

Back at the City Ground on Wednesday, the tension was apparent in a fraught replay bereft of chances and the free flowing football that both teams were capable of producing. That fluidity eluded them as 90 minutes passed without a goal but again it was Birmingham who succeeded in making the breakthrough, this time John Gordon scoring in the 105th minute. Surely Forest were doomed now.

"As Tommy Wilson flicked the ball over I felt it was going to be our last chance," said Roy Dwight, whose lobbed attempt secured another draw and a second replay ten minutes later.

"I decided on a lob and though it cleared Gil Merrick's [the Birmingham goalkeeper] head it seemed to take a long time to drop. It's one goal I'll never forget."

And so to Filbert Street...

Round 5 replay on Wednesday, February 18, at the City Ground, Nottingham Forest: *Thomson; Whare, McDonald; Whitefoot, McKinlay, Burkitt; Dwight, Quigley, Wilson, Gray, Imlach.* Birmingham City: *Merrick; Hall, Allen; Watts, Smith, Neal; Astall, Gordon, Jackson, Larkin, Hooper.* Goal-scorers: *For Forest, Dwight (115). For Birmingham, Gordon (105).* Result: *(after extra time):* Nottingham Forest 1 Birmingham City 1 *Attendance: 39,431*

All change at Leicester – a brief encounter of the third kind

The following Monday, February 23, saw perhaps Forest's finest hour in terms of total football during the 1958/59 season as their incisive, accurate style of play and tidy passing game swept aside Birmingham on the ground of one their fiercest East Midlands rivals. Roy Dwight and Billy Gray cemented a 2-0 interval cushion and Dwight,

SECONDS OUT: A stunning angled effort from Roy Dwight fizzes past Gil Merrick at Filbert Street in the second replay - the winger is on the verge of his hat trick, which he secures two minutes later on the hour, and Forest are on the brink of a sixth round berth

Round 5 second replay on Monday, February 23 at Leicester
Nottingham Forest: *Thomson; Whare, McDonald; Whitefoot, McKinlay, Burkitt; Dwight, Quigley, Wilson, Gray, Imlach.* Birmingham City: *Merrick; Hall, Allen; Watts, Smith, Neal; Astall, Gordon, Orritt, Larkin, Hooper.* Goal-scorers: For Forest, *Dwight (18, 58, 60), Gray (36, 65 penalty)* Result: *Nottingham Forest 5 Birmingham City 0.* Attendance: *34,458*

unplayable on the right wing, claimed a hat trick with two goals in as many minutes just before the hour mark. It was Dwight's second hat trick at Filbert Street that season, having plundered three against Leicester City in a 3-0 win the previous November. When Gray's almost obligatory penalty flew past Gil Merrick in the Birmingham goal in the 65th minute, Birmingham's misery was complete.

Twice the 1959 FA Cup had become almost history to Forest during this fifth round epic. Now it was 5-0 to the team in red. After five hours of pulsating tension and undulating fortunes crammed into nine days, Forest had reached the quarter finals.

SHADES OF GRAY... AGAIN: Billy Gray's third penalty of the competition completes an unlikely, certainly unexpected, rout of Birmingham, runners-up three years before. Gray had earlier scored a more conventional goal as Forest breezed into a 2-0 lead by half time

Chapter 3

Full steam ahead

Holders ousted

TWO days after Birmingham had been humbled at Filbert Street, the city of Nottingham became the victim of a sudden epidemic. The symptoms were relatively painless but sadly incurable and highly contagious. Cup fever had come to town, striking at the core of Forest supporters who desperately wanted to see the current holders Bolton Wanderers at the City Ground this coming Saturday.

FAINT OF HEART: How the Post reported the strain of Cup fever that broke out on the south bank of the River Trent a few days before the quarter final tie

HOUSE FULL: Even from this rare aerial view, clearly it's standing room only in the Trent and Bridgford Ends as a capacity crowd awaits the kick off with Bolton

The Cup ties were coming fast and furious because of Forest's protracted progress but the more games they played, the more the Nottingham public wanted to see their team. Narrow escapes at Tooting, and twice against Birmingham, could only mean one thing. Forest's name was on the trophy and their supporters wanted to share the thrill of the ride all the way to Wembley.

Just as Grimsby had mirrored their advance in the competition to the fourth round, so Bolton's passage to the quarter finals reflected Forest's elongated fifth round route. They too had faced formidable opposition in Lancashire neighbours Preston North End and it required a second replay on neutral ground to settle the tie, 1-0 in their favour.

Mind you, they had beaten the nation's best team in the previous

round, leaving Molineux and the champions elect Wolverhampton Wanderers with a 2-1 victory.

With England centre forward Nat Lofthouse leading the line and captaining the side, Bolton were favourites and there was the added spice concocted by their manager Bill Ridding when the sixth round draw was made initially.

Both teams were involved in replays at the time but Ridding commented that of the two teams he might play should they overcome Preston, he preferred Forest to Birmingham. So now he had been granted his wish, to oppose the supposedly weaker side!

Thus on Wednesday morning at 11am, the selling booths opened at the City Ground to queues of around 8,000 people stretching half a mile

CAPTAINS FULL STRENGTH: The immovable object against the irresistible force. Jack Burkitt meets Nat Lofthouse, the Lion of Vienna

back over Trent Bridge, past the towing path and beyond. The first had arrived at 5.30am that morning, like those that followed desperately eager to secure a ticket for the game.

Schoolboys playing truant and declining to give their names to the Nottingham Evening Post, housewives and widows standing in line for their sons and loyal fans with over 30 years supporting service were among the gathered throng.

At one stage police were called in to restore order as those at the windows buying tickets were crushed by those behind. A number of people fainted, according to some reports, but not the West Bridgford resident who was clearly aggrieved at the subsequent delays as he tried to make his way home for lunch.

"All this for a football match? They must be mad," said angry and tardy of Bread and Lard Island.

Once the curmudgeonly old Bridgfordian with Victor Meldrew tendencies had been removed from the premises, the business of securing a place in the last four began in earnest. Obviously Bolton, as holders, had been there last season although their ultimate success in the Wembley final was tinged with poignancy as they beat a Manchester United side decimated by the Munich air crash. "The most unpopular winners in the

WANDERING NO MORE: Tommy Wilson's effort secured Forest a crucial early lead in the third minute. The Reds never looked back

SAVED... BUT IT'S TOMMY...: With hardly a glint of daylight in the backdrop of the East Stand, opened only two years previously, England goalkeeper Eddie Hopkinson makes a fine save from Roy Dwight's shot...

history of the Cup," was how Lofthouse, scorer of both Bolton goals, one controversial, in the 2-0 win, later reflected.

For Forest, the gap was 57 years, when they last reached the semi finals where they lost to Southampton in 1902.

Astonishingly Forest's largest Saturday crowd had been recorded in the replay win against the amateurs of Tooting and Mitcham, 42,362 emerging from their igloos after the big freeze had immobilised the country.

That figure was eclipsed as a reported 45,000 capacity packaged sardine-like into the City Ground where they saw Tommy Wilson's two goals reflect the home side's enterprise and dashing qualities.

In fact, Forest appeared to continue where they had left off against Birmingham on Monday, coursing with electric touches and invention despite Bolton's solidity at the back. Nat Lofthouse found himself subdued by the polished defending of Bob McKinlay, whose failure to gain a Scottish cap was a mystery to everyone except the tartan-clad selectors in Glasgow and Edinburgh. During an immaculate and distinguished career, unblemished by foul play and untarnished by rude behaviour off the pitch, McKinlay never did win a cap for his country despite some

> *Round 6:*
> *Nottingham Forest v Bolton Wanderers on Saturday, February 28, at the City Ground,*
> Nottingham Forest: *Thomson; Whare McDonald; Whitefoot, McKinlay, Burkitt; Dwight, Quigley, Wilson, Gray, Imlach.*
> Bolton Wanderers: *Hopkinson; Hartle, Banks; Hennin, Edwards, Stanley; Birch, Stevens, Lofthouse, Parry, Holden.*
> Goal-scorers: *For Forest, Wilson (3, 47). For Bolton Wanderers, Birch (62).*
> Result: *Nottingham Forest 2 Bolton Wanderers 1.*
> Attendance: *45,000*

**AT THE DOUBLE:
...but Wilson pounces
for his second two
minutes after the
interval and Forest
are en route to their
first semi final in 57
years**

lamentable excuses for a centre half being favoured with selection in the
blue shirts of Scotland. Mysterious lot north of the border.

With full backs Joe McDonald and Bill Whare effectively blockading
the supply routes from the wings to the great man, Bolton were impotent
against a rampant Forest. True, Brian Birch reduced arrears in the 62nd
minute for the visiting team but Forest prevailed as worthy winners. The
holders had been vanquished in style.

**LION TAMER: Chic
Thomson holds the
rare distinction of
getting the better
of Bolton's fearless
centre forward Nat
Lofthouse in an
aerial duel**

Next stop Wembley

L IFE can be full of coincidences as Forest manager Billy Walker might have concurred on the eve of their semi final with Aston Villa. He was 61 years of age, the same amount of years it was since Forest last won the FA Cup. Their opponents were Aston Villa, with whom he won the Cup as an outstanding player in 1920. And the venue was Hillsborough, home of Sheffield Wednesday, the club he had guided as manager to their third and last FA Cup triumph in 1935.

Could the fates be telling himself something as he stood on the brink of becoming the first manager to steer two different teams to Wembley glory?

In the event, the omens were portentous although they could not predict such a drab contest devoid of skill or grace. Although they had denied Manchester United's star-laden side a historic first Double of the century in 1957 by beating the champions at Wembley amid the furore of Ray Wood's fractured jaw, Villa were a team in decline and destined for relegation at the end of the season.

Thus, a defensive and negative formation awaited Forest, brimming

JACKIE FOILED: Jackie Sewell closes in on Chic Thompson awaiting an error that never came. Villa's England forward paired up with Tommy Lawton at Notts County at the start of the decade to torment Forest in their Third Division days but had moved on to be a Cup winner with the claret and blues via a British record transfer fee of £35,000 to Sheffield Wednesday

PETER PANNED: Peter McParland, his team's two goal hero but Manchester United's villain in Villa's FA Cup win two years previously when he fractured United goalkeeper Ray Wood's jaw in a brutal collision, is among the rough and tumble with Bob McKinlay at Hillsborough

ONLY THE LONELY: The Forest defence appears to have gone AWOL as three Villa attackers including Jackie Sewell and Peter McParland stalk Chic Thomson's goal. Offside surely, linesman?

with confidence from two heady Cup displays against Birmingham and Bolton. As they say, it was not a classic but a collector's item stole the honours and secured the win when Johnny Quigley controlled Tommy Wilson's centre and turned to squeeze an angled shot beyond goalkeeper Nigel Sims as the talented Glaswegian inside forward lay on his backside. Never has a posterior been used to such good effect in the history of the Garibaldi Reds!

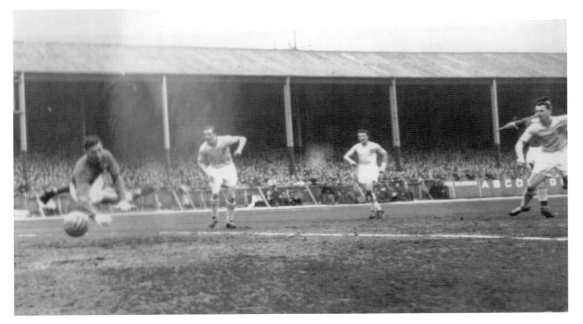

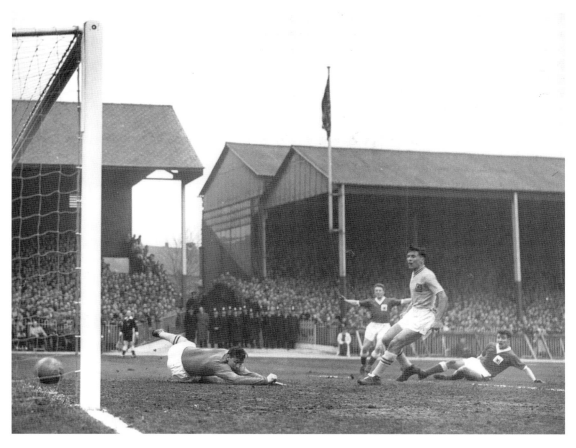

It was the 65th minute with over 65,000 bursting Hillsborough to the seams.

"Villa's defenders let Tommy Wilson's cross come to me," Quigley later reflected. "I was able to bring it to my feet and then let drive for a gap I could see over in the left hand corner. It's difficult to describe your feelings when you score a goal like that."

Rapture, might have been one word to express the emotions of the thousands of Forest fans in South Yorkshire that day.

Perfect timing might have been a couple of others as Quigley troubled the FA Cup scorers for the first time that season. A late but immortal entry into the Forest hall of fame.

JOHNNY COME LATELY: Johnny Quigley, grounded far right, enters the realms of Forest folklore where his name will be forever enshrined with this 65th minute winner that sent the Reds to Wembley. It was his first goal of the season in the competition. How better, and sweeter, late than never! Note the sign of the times in the background as the South Yorkshire Constabulary savour the moment without so much as an 'evenin' all' to the capacity audience.

Semi-Final: Nottingham Forest v Aston Villa, on Saturday, March 14 at Sheffield.
Nottingham Forest: *Thomson; Whare, McDonald; Whitefoot, McKinlay, Burkitt; Dwight, Quigley, Wilson, Gray, Imlach.*
Aston Villa: *Sims; Aldis, Winston; Dixon, Dugdale, Crowe; Smith, Sewell, Hitches, Wylie, McParland.*
Goal-scorers: For Forest, *Quigley (65).*
Result: *Nottingham Forest 1 Aston Villa 0.*
Attendance: *65,107*

Chapter 4

Final countdown

Redmayne and Todd and more double acts

EVERYONE wanted to get in on the act, and not only Redmayne and Todd, the local specialists in sports equipment who catered for athletes of all sizes and gender from the hockey pitches of the High School on Valley Road to the oche at the Barley Mow in Basford.

Its retail outlet, housed in the magnificent Victorian emporium on the corner of Carrington Street and Canal Street, was a majestic presence amid the grimier Broad and Narrow Marsh areas and stood smartly to attention as an impressive welcome as part of the gateway into the city from the nearby Midland Station.

Just a short bike or trolley bus ride from the City Ground or Trent Bridge, it was also a handy distance for professional footballers from both

COVERED FROM HEAD TO TOE: Sponsors were just as keen then to get their names on a football kit and the FA Cup Final. With its live television audience increasing with each passing year, it presented a unique opportunity for brand awareness. Redmayne and Todd supplied the goods, the tracksuits, the full Forest strip and boots and shinpads with manufacturers Umbro and Adidas being the main beneficiaries of a 'commercial plug' about which admen fantasized. Harold Alcock is seen testing the bend factor in the boots along with Billy Walker and a Redmayne representative for a City Ground photo call. The other image shows Redmayne's shop window frontage in the weeks before May 2

sides of the Trent to drop in and choose a new pair of boots.

While the cricketers headed for that other fabled pairing of Gunn and Moore, manufacturers of the willow almost by regal appointment, it was the rank and file from Notts County and Nottingham Forest whose patronage was endemic in Redmayne's culture. A philosophy of 'good enough for the pros, good enough for the amateurs' who enjoyed their 90 minutes of relative fame in the flourishing grass roots of the Notts

COLLAR AND TIE AFFAIR: Already booted, now suited. Tommy Wilson, Jeff Whitefoot, Jack Burkitt and Bob McKinlay are among the players surveying the shirts and ties, presented by the dapper chap third from right of Billy Walker, that formed part of the traditional Wembley suit on the big day

1898   REDMAYNE'S   1959

SUPPLY IT!

The

F.A. CUP FINAL OUTFIT

WORN BY

NOTTINGHAM FOREST F.C.

Send for the Sporting Broadsheet

REDMAYNE & TODD LTD.

CARRINGTON STREET

NOTTINGHAM

BRANCHES AT — LEICESTER   BURTON   OLDBURY   LOUTH

THE OLDEST PROFESSION: Currying the populist vote by championing a good sporting thing from elected offices is a political tradition still observed with immaculate timing and sycophancy today

THE LORD MAYOR'S PARLOUR,
THE COUNCIL HOUSE,
NOTTINGHAM.

TEL. No. 44331.

26th March, 1959

After a lapse of 61 years Nottingham Forest Football Club has brought a signal honour to the City, which is taking immense pride in having one of its teams in the F.A. Cup Final.

Credit is due to all the members of the team, its manager, Mr. W. H. Walker, and its Committee.

This souvenir booklet serves as a means of showing Nottingham's sportsmen's appreciation and will serve, too, to mark in tangible form what people think of Nottingham's distinguished footballers. Good luck to them at Wembley.

J. W. Littlefair,
Lord Mayor of Nottingham.

Good Luck Message from the Lord Mayor of Nottingham

Ask for it by Name!

AT YOUR CO·OP STORE

NUTTY-

SUNSHINE SLIC
AMERICAN TY

NUTT

SUNSHINE SLICED

The N.C.S. Bakery offers 22 varieties of good, fresh bread, latest winner being the new Vienna baps, ovals and sticks. They're just the thing to add mealtime magic to your tea-table, and only 6d.

Enriched with added butter, sugar and milk to give extra flavour and extra nourishment, Nutty Crust is the best loaf you can buy, well worth the extra coppers. Try some, today!

NUTTY-CRUST

American-
style
Milk Loaf.

Exclusive to NOTTINGHAM CO-OPERATIVE SOCIETY Shops, Supermarkets and Vans

THE FINAL CHOICE

The 'Wonderloaf' TRADE MARK

MADE PURELY FOR YOU !

by *Blanchards* (BAKERS) LTD.

WATNALL, NOTTM.

Alliance, Midland Amateur Alliance and the Notts Thursday League, among many others.

Thus, with signed chitty in hand, a famous legacy of players had passed through its doors from Wally Ardron to Tommy Lawton, all seeking footwear that resembled hobnail boots more suited for colliers, supported by wooden studs and lashings of dubbin to soften the virtually intractable leather.

Redmayne's had been supplying the city's clubs at every level for a good many years before the legendary Lawton and Ardron passed through their doors. Since 1898 in fact, the year Forest won their first FA Cup at

BREAD AND BUTTER: Loafing around the bookies remains a time-honoured ritual for professional footballers. No longer snooker halls. However, reflecting that sporting betrayal of a misspent youth in those days, Howarth Nuttall and Sons, for all your billiards room requirements and repairs, wished the boys well later in the same special supplement

INTERNATIONAL BOXING PROMOTER
AND TURF ACCOUNTANT

REG KING

WISHES FOREST
ALL THE BEST AT WEMBLEY

The Nottingham Forest Football Club who brought back the Cup in 1898

Mr. H. Hallam (*Secretary*), Frank Forman, A. Ritchie, D. Allsopp, J. McPherson, W. Wragg, A. Scott, G. Bee (*Trainer*),
T. McInnes, C. H. Richards, L. Benbow, A. Capes, A. Spouncer.

THE BEST PICTURES . . . THE BEST REPORT
in the
SUNDAY EXPRESS
CUP FINAL SPECIAL

PAPER TALK: The victors of the past share space with the present and the national newspapers rightly wanted a share of the action although Jack Burkitt, the Forest captain, would have been paid a pittance in comparison, to today's ghosted columns for his views in The People on Sunday. Burkitt was the stoic figure at the hub of Forest's resurgence but his talents, lauded by his peers, were never recognised by the England selectors at international level. Joe Mercer, the defeated Villa manager in the semi finals, echoed the thoughts of the majority when he expressed dismay and bafflement as to why the skipper had never been capped at full international level by his country. Charles Buchan and his iconic Football Monthly agreed

Don't miss the grand
CUP FINAL SOUVENIR
in the new issue of
CHARLES BUCHAN'S
FOOTBALL MONTHLY
Ask the newsagent for **YOUR** copy to-day

★ Pictures of star players in full colour

★ Why Forest Will Win at Wembley, by Charles Buchan (exclusive)

JACK BURKITT
writes for THE PEOPLE

Jack Burkitt, Forest's brilliant skipper, is writing exclusively in THE PEOPLE. In his own words he'll tell you about Forest's exciting fight to Wembley — and the real inside stories before and after the Cup Final. It's a must for every fan. Don't miss a single word of this tremendous scoop — ask your newsagent to deliver THE PEOPLE every Sunday.

All the Inside Stories on Sport!

No other newspaper brings you such brilliant and comprehensive sports coverage as THE PEOPLE! The inside stories...boardroom secrets...they're all scooped in THE PEOPLE!

- **SOCCER CHATTER** by Joe Hulme and Harry Peterson.
- **SOCCER BETTING** by Ralph Hadley.
- **BEST AND FULLEST REPORTS.**
- **FIGHTING TALK** — Ernie Jarvis on boxing.
- **LARRY LYNX** to help you beat the bookies.

EXCLUSIVELY IN
THE PEOPLE
ON SUNDAY

PLAYERS PLEASE: Enough to reduce today's nanny state to one of apoplexy, England's largest cigarette producer with its industrial base in Nottingham encourages the young and able to have a drag with a medium Navy Cut in an era when smoke got in everyone's eyes in the dressing room. Opposite, the mighty Radio Times

PLAYER'S
Britain's best liked cigarettes

They taste better - *that's why*

NOTTINGHAM is proud of her PLAYERS

Ahead for Quality

SENIOR SERVICE *Satisfy*

WELL MADE · WELL PACKED

Crystal Palace, against Derby County, so how apposite that they should be on hand to cater for Forest's needs the second time around.

Actually, a glance at the advertising space and sponsored messages of goodwill in a variety of local publications confirm the dichotomy of the passing years, at least in this neck of the woods.

How vastly times have changed in the actual establishments and institutions that were forged into the Nottingham landscape yet how some things have not altered in the slightest in what attracts professional footballers, or at least the perception of it.

If someone was asked to summarise the

You're bound to miss something without

RADIO TIMES

FULL BBC TELEVISION AND SOUND PROGRAMMES

EVERY FRIDAY   FOURPENCE

CRACKERJACK! Can you spot the Peter Glaze lookalike on the Forest committee? There must be at least three contenders. Harold Alcock takes centre stage of a group of men who appear more like the Tory Cabinet vainly trying to execute an informal pose before heading off on their holidays

predominant themes over the ensuing pages in terms of a plot for a modern day television soap, high among the script would be fast cars, slow horses, fashion icons and the inevitable twin vices or peaks depending on opinion, of hard liqueur and heavy drinking. Throw in a tap room or lounge bar immersed in tobacco smoke and it's just another day in the Rovers Return, at least before New Labour began dictating lifestyle from its political pulpit.

Strangely enough the Forest squad of 1959 would claim empathy with the clientele at the Rovers Return just as their Wembley successors half a century later would identify more with the opulence of say Dallas or Dynasty in the trashy soap realm.

From the staff of life, provided by the Wonderloaf of Watnall's Blanchards Bakery and the Co-op's Nutty Crust to Reg King, boxing promoter and doubtless genial turf accountant, there are rich, sumptuous slices of 1950s Nottingham, its values and its society that reflect a certain gentility in comparison to the current climate. Rose-tinted glasses may invoke a nostalgic hue clouded by the passage of time but who would deny the absurd charm of Mr Stanley, flatterer of hair in New York, Paris and Amsterdam and also 52A Long Row.

Worth a visit out of idle curiosity alone as well as a trip to T. Stevenson, on Alfreton Road, who as a bookmaker of that parish promises to be 'liberal, fair and reliable' which in the long history of syntax must be the first time an amalgam of those three words have appeared in a bookies' promotional charter.

Wines - Spirits - Bottled Beer
Liqueurs - Cigars - Flowers

★
★ ★
★

SKINNER & ROOK

★
★

17a CLUMBER STREET
NOTTINGHAM

Telephone: Nottingham 44504

★
★ ★
★

★ *where fine Wines
cost as little as 6/6 a bottle !*

Two popular favourites !

"The FOREST" and SHIPSTONE'S ALE

SHIPSTONE - STAR BREWER...

Phone: 54109

The Square

Sole Proprietor: L. Atkin

OFF-LICENCE BEERS AND STOUT
RETAILER WINES AND SPIRITS

Wine & Spirit Stores

**Commercial Square
80-82 St. Ann's Well Road
Nottingham**

Also 776 Mansfield Road, Woodthorpe · Tel. 26-7638

THE BLACK DEATH: Shipstone's had as many nicknames as it had detractors, many times both in anguished harmony on a Sunday morning after the Saturday night before in the public bar or on the Arkwright Street run of insurmountable tap rooms. The Black Death might have been a tad melodramatic, even for Shippo's and when the local brewery finally shut, it was mourned by even its fiercest critics. Other brews and alcohol dispensing establishments, including the fabled Skinner and Rook, reflected a drinking culture frowned upon today both in the game and society. Over the page, one of its pioneers or leading lights back then was the inimitable and gifted Jimmy Greaves, clearly weaned on Bovril before graduating to the harder stuff. Small wonder that the virtuous Andrews, for 'inner cleanliness' was such a popular seller

Jimmy Greaves in action at Stamford Bridge.

Read what England's top teenage player says about Bovril

Chelsea's dynamic inside forward, 19-year-old Jimmy Greaves, has already made his mark in league football.

He was one of the youngest players ever chosen for the England Under-23 International team. Many will remember his first sensational goal for that team in 1957. Within the first ten minutes of his first match Jimmy Greaves had scored. He has maintained his early promise in being one of the leading goal scorers in the Football League.

Jimmy, the most proficient teenage player in this country today, trains and wins on Bovril. He says, "Like many other professional footballers, I take Bovril regularly all through the season. I thoroughly enjoy it – wouldn't be without it in fact. Bovril is a big help in keeping you feeling at the top of your form."

BOVRIL does you a power of good

Are you on the ball?

Or isn't your inside right?

Like a gormless goalie with a greasy ball—are you forever fumbling with life—letting opportunities slip through your fingers? Or like a sleep-walking centre forward, do you lack the drive to reach your goal?

When your left half doesn't seem to know what your right half is doing and your better half starts barracking—it's time to call half time and take stock of the situation. Life need not seem like a crazy game, nor need you feel so foul.

All that is required is a daily workout for your metabolism—in other words, a little Andrews every morning.

It will restore your energy, your drive, your initiative—and strengthen your defences.

Andrews in the morning makes it a great day—right from the kick off!

ANDREWS FOR _INNER_ CLEANLINESS

MEN AND MOTORS: The Aston Martin DB6 or the Ferrari? It's a tough choice for today's modern footballer when he's reached a Wembley Final. And that's just for the missus. Still, fast cars, or at least sluggish, middle-range beasts with a 0-60mph measured in calendar days, could turn a young player's head even though many of them cycled to or caught a bus and from work. The Vauxhall Victor De-Luxe, Series II, on sale at dealer's Oscroft's, was one such eye-catcher. Only £565, plus purchase tax of £236-10-10d. Full price £801-10-10d (or £801-54p in post L-s-d currency approx)

FOR YOUR **FINAL** CHOICE

Choose Austin

The New Austin A.55

Available for demonstration from the distributors

ATKEY'S OF NOTTM LTD

20 LOWER PARLIAMENT ST. NOTTINGHAM   Tel. 53574

WHEN TALKING OF CARS

IT COSTS NOTHING

to visit our extensive salerooms and discuss your requirements without obligation.

Remember a little skilled advice can save you £ £ £'s, and there's no obligation to purchase at—

LADY BAY GARAGE

Official Ford Dealers

RADCLIFFE ROAD, WEST BRIDGFORD, NOTTINGHAM

Phone 84971 and 84409

Always a large and comprehensive stock of GUARANTEED USED CARS

in our showroom now The Series II **VICTOR DE-LUXE**

All the glamour and prestige of a true luxury car for a basic £565 ! Individual front seats, fine quality leather upholstery deep pile carpets, dual or single colours. Victor roadability, performance and economy, with the new Series 2 look of the future. See it today . . . try it for yourself.

Oscroft's

£565

P.T. £236 . 10 . 10

Total £801 . 10 . 10

CASTLE BOULEVARD NOTTINGHAM - Phone 45027

NOW OPEN 8 a.m. to 8 p.m.

—WORLD'S FINEST FOOTBALL BOOTS!

They're lightweight, streamlined, flexible—they're designed by Stanley Matthews, the world's most famous footballer.

FOOTBALL BOOTS

All sizes for men, youths, and boys, obtainable only from **FOOTWEAR DEPARTMENT, CHURCH STREET** and branch stores of

MANSFIELD SUTTON & DISTRICT CO-OPERATIVE SOCIETY Ltd.

Mr. Stanley

The flatterer of

hair

PARIS   NEW YORK   AMSTERDAM

Stanley Barber International Hair Fashion
52A LONG ROW WEST END
NOTTINGHAM

ANOTHER FINE MESS: Never have two Stanleys been so diametrically opposed in their endeavours. You might think

May We Recommend..

. . . THAT YOU ENJOY THE CASUAL COMFORT, AND THE PERFECTLY BLENDED COLOURS OF A SPORTS JACKET OR TWO-PIECE SUIT SELECTED FROM OUR VERY WIDE RANGE.

TRINITY SQUARE
NOTTINGHAM
— TELEPHONE 46251 —

Will Hill

A reliable and fair racing service
S.P. or Tote

T. STEVENSON

102 Alfreton Road, Nottingham

Telephones 74574-5-6-7-8 and 74398

| BOOKS OPEN ON ALL FUTURE EVENTS | LIBERAL COMMISSION TO AGENTS | CREDIT ACCOUNTS ARRANGED |

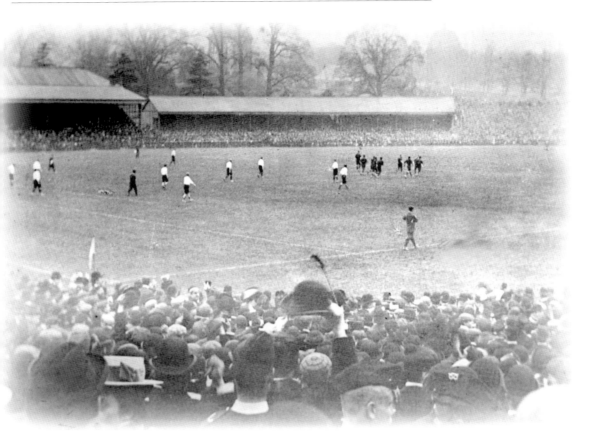

Campbell Bros.
(Nottm.) **LTD.**
6a LOWER PARLIAMENT STREET,
NOTTINGHAM

Famous since
1899

The oldest firm
of turf accountants
in Nottingham
offers Nottm. Forest
good wishes for
Wembley.

NAGS BY A SHORT HEAD: A selection of Nottingham's finest bookies, including the oldest Campbell Bros who arrived just a year too late to open a book on Forest's previous final at the Crystal Palace.

GONE TO SUPERMARKETS NEARLY EVERY ONE: Fashion, food, news, sports and leisure wear, just a few of the Nottingham landmarks that are gone but largely not forgotten including the Aladdin's cave of magazines and foreign newspapers that was Briddock's on Upper Parliament Street. Watson Fothergill's Black Boy was perhaps the most lamentable casualty. In its distinguished lifetime it housed Gregory Peck and Don Bradman's touring Aussies who asked for Little John, the clock's bell in its dome tower, to be silenced so his players could sleep on the eve of an Ashes game at Trent Bridge. The City Council in the 1960s pushed for its demolition, replacing the grand Victorian design and architecture with a red-brick supermarket store frontage that is Primark today

BANQUETING ROOMS
BOARD MEETINGS
BOUNTIFUL FOOD
BEAUTIFUL BEER
AND THE
BEST OF EVERYTHING

AT THE

**BLACK BOY
HOTEL**

(Nottingham 41531)

The Name to remember!

William Gunn

"AUTOGRAPH"
hand-made BATS
Also "CANNON" "VELHIDE DRIVER"
in all sizes
All accessories for Cricket including
BALLS, LEG GUARDS, PROTECTORS,
GLOVES, FOOTWEAR, CLOTHING,
GROUND EQUIPMENT, Etc.

Send for
FREE
CATALOGUE

REPAIRS & RE-
BLADING of ALL
MAKES a speciality.

Agents for NOTTS.
RED MARL the finest
top dressing for turf.

Be sure your TENNIS RACKET is a winner!

Choose from our Stock
GLEAVES
Whipshaft County £7.15.3
DUNLOP
Maxply Fort £7.15.3
Others from £2.9.9
SLAZENGER
Challenge Power (Blue Spot) £7.15.3
Others from £2.11.0
GUNN & MOORE
Portland De-luxe £6.4.0
GRAYS, SPALDINGS RACKETS
from . . . £2.8.3
24 hr. Restringing & Repair Service

Established
in 1885

GUNN & MOORE LTD
49 CARRINGTON ST. NOTTINGHAM
Telephone: 55923/4

Freda Hoole's

County
SALON
ladies hair artists of distinction

BURTON STREET
NOTTINGHAM

*Look out for the opening
of her modern salon*

at   BURTON CHAMBERS
FRIAR LANE

All Sportsmen read—

Focus on Sport
by A. J. TURNER

in the

WEST BRIDGFORD
and
CLIFTON STANDARD

Published every Friday

Circulating in West Bridgford, Clifton,
Ruddington, Wilford, Keyworth, Gotham
and surrounding district

WHEN IT COMES TO FINE FOODS

La Ronde Restaurant

29 MANSFIELD ROAD
NOTTINGHAM

TEL. 43668

IS RIGHT ON THE BALL

"*Bringing you the news*
you ought
to know—"

BRIDDOCKS
THE CITY'S NEWSPAPER SHOP
UPPER PARLIAMENT STREET
TELEPHONE 41167
We are open Sunday Mornings from 8.30—12.30

It's the *ITALIAN* Line for '59

● There's ease and comfort in this all-wool cavalry twill suit. Style too, in the centre-vent jacket, with flap ticket pockets. 19" width trousers have cross pockets. The price?

£9.19.6

● London-tailored in the Italian style, with the high three-button jacket, continental collar, slit pockets, all giving the popular extra-slim look. At a slim price too, only

£7.19.0

● Co-operative House 'made to measure' tailoring is un-rivalled, with widest choice of styles and finest cloths, and a perfect fit guaranteed at prices from

13 gns. & 15 gns.

WEATHER OUTLOOK

It's fine now, but rainy days are bound to come! Be well equipped with a CO-OP handy POCKET MAC priced from **9/11**

UPPER PARLIAMENT STREET, NOTTINGHAM and BRANCHES

Nottingham Co-operative Society Limited

And the ref was called Clough

LETTERS OF INTENT: Redmayne and Todd are confident Forest will be the smartest team to have graced the Wembley turf, sartorially speaking that is. The BBC Midlands Home Service contract proffering the princely sum of £1 11s 6d for an interview with Harold Alcock and the details of their Signpost to Wembley feature programme

AS the days dwindled away before the Final tie, so the pre-match blurb intensified but soon it dawned upon Forest fans that here indeed, was a historic day for them all to enjoy. The pundits were not so keen, however, and the media, with a southern bias, dismissed the two protagonists as uninteresting or dreary.

There was, after all, no capital clubs involved, the champions Wolverhampton Wanderers had been knocked out by Bolton and none of the other northern giants had survived to the ultimate stage. Manchester United typically led that latter pack but had fallen at the first attempt to Norwich City, themselves the giant killing tour de force of the competition that season, beating

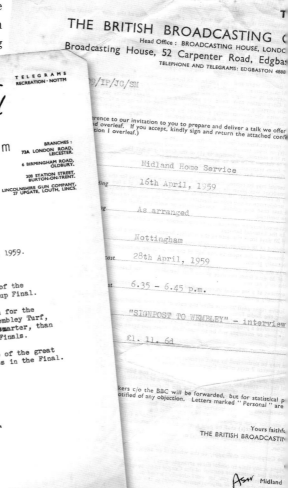

THE BRITISH BROADCASTING CORPORATION

Head Office : Broadcasting House, London, W.1

Bentinck Buildings, Wheeler Gate, Nottingham

TELEPHONES AND TELEGRAMS : NOTTINGHAM 44754 AND 44773

8th April, 1959.

H.W. Alcock, Esq.,
12 Stamford Road,
West Bridgford,
Nottingham.

Dear Mr. Alcock,

We have met many times at the Council House and other places. This is to tell you that we are putting out a BBC sound programme about Nottingham Forest called "Signpost to Wembley", on April 28th (our regular weekly spot, in fact, re-christened for the occasion). We shall not be talking about playing tactics and so forth, but about the background to the whole problem of being in the Cup Final club. I would very much like you to do a very short recording – not more than a minute – as Chairman of the club, about how the ticket allocation is working out, and perhaps about your own problems of dodging the people who are, no doubt, pestering you to death. Messrs. Walker, Burkitt, Mr. Porter, the Deputy Chief Constable, and others will be taking part.

I think it would be ~~entirely wrong~~ *a pity* to put out a programme without a word from the Chairman, and I should be grateful if you would get in touch with me by telephone for preference, to fix a time when you could come in to do this quite simple piece of speaking.

Yours sincerely,

Gerald Nethercot

(Gerald Nethercot)
East Midlands Representative

P.S. Mr. Porter is coming in at 10.45 tomorrow, Thursday, to do his part. If you could come in at the same time that would be helpful, but if not then let me know when it will be convenient.

BW

BLACK AND WHITE AND RED ALL OVER: One of the many special supplements that preceded Forest's Wembley appearance

Tottenham Hotspur and Blackpool from the top flight before the third division side succumbed to Billy Bingham's late goal in the semi final replay at St Andrew's.

No other football competition gripped any country like the FA Cup back then and for the players it was an opportunity to have their status

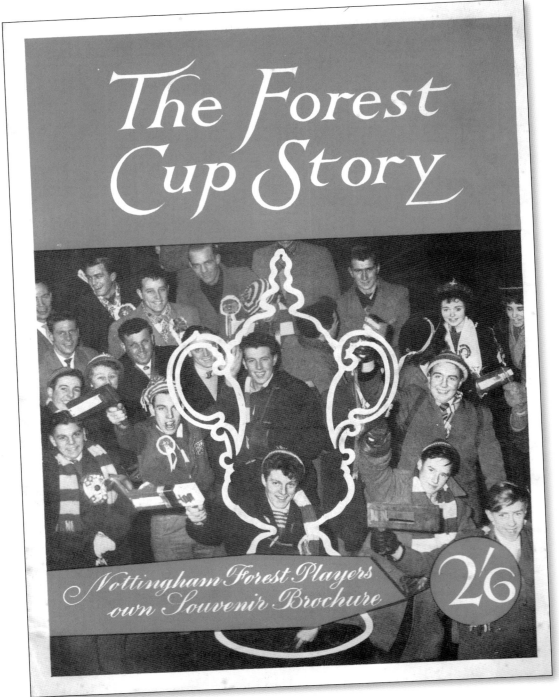

The Forest Cup Story

Nottingham Forest Players own Souvenir Brochure

2/6

ROOM ON TOP:
On the buses or on
the trains, Reds
supporters found a
way to Wembley

elevated and to become, for 90 minutes at the very least, a household name.
On the Wembley turf, legends and folklore could be written but before that
there was the players' pool and the chance to earn a few bob more than the
maximum wage of around £20 a week.

For most finalists, ticket allocation was crucial. Players freely sold
theirs for several times the face value, an accepted dressing room practice
to which clubs turned a blind eye, especially as Cup and win bonuses
were frugal at best, as little as £4 for victory in the league depending on
attendance.

Thus this was an important cash bonanza for professionals and there
were the usual mumbles and grumbles in the squad, particularly when
details of the post match banquet emerged, demanding that reserve players
had to return home by the last train from London on Saturday night.

It was a brief skirmish in the national papers, swiftly smoothed
over by Forest who admitted an oversight and misunderstanding. A rare
victory for player power but a portentous one as the decade came to a close,
ushering in the 1960s, George Best and a new era for the beautiful game.

PLANNING CONSENT: The official, really official, Forest itinerary and Cup Final arrangements, the latter as decreed by Sir Stanley Rous, secretary of the FA no less. Forest's movements included a decamp to Brighton on Sunday and return to Nottingham via St Pancras on Monday, with the ladies leaving a little earlier. The FA's precise instructions demanded that at:

i) 2.48pm: The players must be ready to leave the dressing rooms. A member of the FA Staff – Mr H N Bird – will inform... when to leave

ii) the interval of the tie must not exceed 10 minutes

And at the final whistle after the presentation of the Cup in the Royal Box:

iii) A member of the FA Staff Mr Bird (for it is he again) ...will direct these movements. Immediately after the second linesman has joined the players, the National Anthem will be played, Sir Stanley Rous, who will be standing beside Her Majesty, will give the signal to the Bandmaster.

In fact the ubiquitous Mr H N Bird, not be confused with HRH Prince Philip, was very much in attendance throughout most of the day, lunching with the referee and linesman as well as arranging their transport from Lancaster Gate

NOTTINGHAM FOREST

FOOTBALL CLUB

Itinerary

F.A. CUP FINAL

SATURDAY, MAY 2nd, 1959

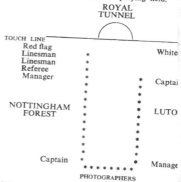

Their Royal Highnesses The Prince Philip, burgh, and The Duke of Gloucester, th Team at the white flag, and the Nottingham at the red flag. The referee and linesmen w positions as indicated in the diagram below. will supervise these arrangements. Photographers must wait until after the tea tion before they enter the playing field.

ROYAL
TUNNEL

TOUCH LINE
Red flag
Linesman — White
Linesman
Referee
Manager — Captai

NOTTINGHAM
FOREST — LUTO

Captain — Manage

PHOTOGRAPHERS

When Their Royal Highnesses reach the tou National Anthem will be played. After the pres players may "kick-about" until the Referee calls together to toss for ends. The Referee must not sta until Their Royal Highnesses are seated in the Roy

3.00 p.m. Kick-off.

3.45 p.m. Half time. The players will leave the f interval must not exceed 10 minutes. Immediately the match is over, the players ar match officials will assemble in front of the Ro Uniformed attendants will remove about 10 the front row of the Royal Box to facilitate th tion of the Cup and Medals.

2

SECTION III

Footballs and Linesmen's Flags.

The Footballs will be supplied by a few have instructions to deliver a ball, witho Offices of the Association on the day of have been informed that they must not cc match officials or officials of the competing the fact that they are submitting a ball.

Mr. W. R. Osborne will be responsible balls and flags to Wembley and for taking t dressing room for the referee to make his choice has been made at the Offices of Th tion on the morning of the match. The p taken by Mr. Osborne to the respective dr the match. During the game these will be i trainers and after the match they will be trainers by Mr. Osborne for return to Lan

Cup and Medals.

Mr. Osborne will deliver the Cup and Me n arrival at Wembley. At 4.30 p.m., Wer ring them to the Royal Box.

SECTION IV

Ball Boys.

The ball-boys have been nominated by the A. and a Steward will be in charge of port to him at the Empire Pool, Wemble noon, and be under his charge. They h passes for the match and refreshments fore and after the match and at half-time. The boys will enter the Arena from the mediately after the teams have been prese During the presentation of the M sition behind the

2.50 p.m. Her Majesty The Queen and The Duke of Edinburgh, will arrive at the will be received by the President, H.R.H. ester, who will present the officials named

2.53 p.m., after the presentations, Her Maj be escorted by Sir Leslie Bowker (Vice-C to the Royal Box. H.R.H. Prince Philip burgh and H.R.H. The Duke of Gloucest e playing pitch. The Bandmaster will recei Stanley Rous to play the National Anthen Majesty The Queen into the Royal Box a the touch line will

Patron:
HER MAJESTY THE QUEEN
President:
H.R.H. THE DUKE OF GLOUCESTER, K.G., K.T.
Secretary: *Chairman of the Council:*
SIR STANLEY ROUS, C.B.E., J.P.   A. DREWRY, ESQ., C.B.E., J.P.

THE FOOTBALL ASSOCIATION CHALLENGE CUP COMPETITION

FINAL TIE

LUTON TOWN F.C.

V.

NOTTINGHAM FOREST F.C.

THE EMPIRE STADIUM, WEMBLEY

ON

SATURDAY, 2ND MAY, 1959

KICK-OFF at 3 p.m.

Programme of Arrangements

THE FOOTBALL ASSOCIATION CHALLENGE CUP COMPETITION

FINAL TIE
LUTON TOWN
v
NOTTINGHAM FOREST

SATURDAY, MAY 2nd, 1959   KICK-OFF 3 pm

EMPIRE STADIUM
WEMBLEY

OFFICIAL PROGRAMME   ·   ONE SHILLING

BOB A JOB: The symbolic Cup Final programme that was a design classic for a generation of Wembley ties. Price One shilling

THE GENTLE TOUCH : The Forest players' wives appear dressed more for tea and digestives in the front parlour rather than a racy night out in a nightclub's VIP lounge or indeed the fashion parade opportunity that the FA Cup Final now represents for Premier League totty. Still, the first ladies of 1959 evoked the current vogue of sorts -- and a touch of sedate class lacking in most of the modern equivalent

 # LUTON TOWN

(White Shirts, Black Shorts)

Goal
R. BAYNHAM

2
Right Back
B. McNALLY

3
Left Back
K. HAWKES

4
Right Half
J. GROVES

5
Centre Half
S. OWEN (Capt.)

6
Left Half
D. PACEY

8
Inside Right
A. BROWN

10
Inside Left
G. CUMMINS

7
Outside Right
W. BINGHAM

9
Centre Forward
R. MORTON

11
Outside Left
T. GREGORY

Referee
J. CLOUGH
(Lancashire)

Linesmen:
Major C. H. DENNIS (Army)
Orange Flag
G. E. READLE (Manchester)
Flame Flag

11
Outside Left
S. IMLACH

9
Centre Forward
T. WILSON

7
Outside Right
R. DWIGHT

10
Inside Left
W. GRAY

8
Inside Right
J. QUIGLEY

6
Left Half
J. BURKITT (Capt.)

5
Centre Half
R. McKINLAY

4
Right Half
J. WHITEFOOT

3
Left Back
J. McDONALD

2
Right Back
W. WHARE

Goal
C. THOMSON

 # NOTTINGHAM FOREST

(Red Shirts, White Shorts)

ANY CHANGES IN THE ABOVE TEAMS WILL BE ANNOUNCED

"Reds" make Wembley Debut

By Harry Richards

FEW clubs can boast a more colourful background than Nottingham Forest, proudly making their first appearance at Wembley this afternoon.

Throughout the history of the game the name of this Midland club, which had modest beginnings, continually crops up. It is safe to say that at the present time they are enjoying their most successful period ever under the managership of Mr. Billy Walker who, both as a player and administrator, has given much to football.

Forest, known by their supporters as "The Reds," came into existence as long ago as 1865, being the third oldest club in the country, near neighbours Notts County being the first, followed by Stoke City.

It was in 1865 that a number of Nottingham youths, who played shinney—a crude form of hockey—decided to form a football club. For a short time the club played shinney and football, but then they decided to concentrate on soccer and became Nottingham Forest F.C., the name being derived from the fact that their pitch was on a recreation ground known as "the forest."

Forest have made many valuable contributions to the game. In 1874, a famous wearer of their Garibaldi red shirt, Samuel Weller Widdowson—his father was a lover of Charles Dickens' books—invented shinguards. Four years later the referee's whistle was used for the first time in a match between Forest and Sheffield Norfolk at Nottingham.

Quickly the Forest achieved fame. They beat many of the best teams in the country, competed for the F.A. Cup for the first time in 1878–79 and reached the semi-final at the first attempt—a feat which remains a record.

● "SEMI" IN SCOTLAND

In 1884–85 Forest figured in the only F.A. Cup semi-final ever played in Scotland, losing to Queen's Park in a replay at Edinburgh.

The Reds were represented at the inaugural meeting of the Football League in 1888, but they did not become one of the original 12 founder clubs, only because they could not obtain fixtures.

Forest joined the Football Alliance and soon won the Championship. Then came the extension of the First Division of the Football League and the start of Division Two. The Midland side were elected to the senior division.

They are also proud of the fact that they helped to give Arsenal a start in 1886. One of their players migrated to Woolwich and when it was decided to form "Royal Arsenal," Forest provided the shirts. That is the reason the Gunners adopted red on their colours.

Mr. Walker, who celebrated 20 years at the City ground this year, has had much to do with the club's emergence as one of the best footballing sides in the country.

The former Villa and England inside left—he holds a Cup Winner's and a Loser's medal, and managed Sheffield Wednesday when they won the trophy in 1935—remains the only manager still with the club he controlled before the war.

He has always had the enthusiastic support of the club committee. To many people the use of the word "committee" may sound strange, but it is a fact that Forest are unique in this particular, too. **They are not a limited company, which means that they have no board of directors.** The club are very proud of the fact that they are run by a committee and in this respect stand alone.

It is the proud boast of all connected with the club that Nottingham Forest—they abhor being called Notts Forest—have got together the best side ever to represent them. **This is high praise indeed when it is realised that in another six years the club will be celebrating its century.**

HISTORY MAN: Harry Richards, of the Nottingham Evening Post, proclaims Forest's first visit to Wembley with a few nuggets from the club's past

THE WAY THEY WERE: Opposite, the line-ups, numbers 1-11 only, as shown in the Wembley programme

COME ON YOU REDS: Are they bobby sockers giving everyone a twirl? A generation on and the handbags on the bottom right of the picture would later be used as a central focus point to dance around at discos

LUTON TOWN F.C. 1958-59

[Photo by courtesy *Home Counties Newspapers, Ltd.*]

Back Row (*left to right*) : FRANK KING (*Trainer*), JOHN GROVES, BRENDAN McNALLY, RON BAYNHAM, DAVE PACEY, KEN HAWKES
Front Row (*left to right*) : BILLY BINGHAM, ALLAN BROWN, SID OWEN, BOB MORTON, GEORGE CUMMINS, TONY GREGORY

BRING ME SUNSHINE: As Luton Town's most famous supporter might have said of his team. The sun came out; sadly not the shine. Eric Morecambe's lament, playing all the right notes, but not necessarily in the right order, applied to his beloved Hatters that day

BROWN SEES RED - EVENTUALLY: Captain Syd Owen makes the introductions to Allan Brown, scorer of a fourth round hat trick against Leicester City at Kenilworth Road. Brown returned to manage Luton and later he took charge of Forest, succeeding Dave Mackay at the City Ground, although his tenure is best recalled for its ending, his departure making way for one Brian Clough in January 1975

GRAND ENTRANCE: The teams experience that Wembley 'roar' for the first time as they make that familiar walk in Indian file towards a regal appointment in the shadow of the Royal Box

SCOT'S BROTH: Prince Philip meets Chic Thomson... "not another bloody Scot" the normally diplomatic Duke of Edinburgh opined to Forest's Perth-born goalkeeper, he being the fifth Scotsman in their starting XI that the Prince had encountered. In all, there were 12 players of the tartan persuasion on Forest's books at the time

BREAK A LEG: Fortunately the Prince, despite the Royals' patronage and indulgence of the thespian set, is unlikely to have delivered that line to Roy Dwight

The Wembley wonders of 1959

Top row from left:
TOM GRAHAM (trainer) – the 'father confessor' to the players, the England centre half honed his talents in County Durham before joining Forest in 1927 where he stayed on... and on. Appointed trainer in 1944, a trusted and vital ally to the manager during Forest's gradual rise to the highest levels of the domestic game

JOE McDONALD –joined Forest at the start of the season from Sunderland and swiftly replaced veteran Geoff Thomas at left back. A cultured ball player, an incongruous trait for defenders of that era, he represented both Scotland and Great Britain. Something of a wise cracking joker in the pack, he faltered twice at the semi final stage with the Wearsiders while playing alongside Billy Bingham, Luton's most dangerous attacker who he marked so closely at Wembley. Aspired to be a sewing machine mechanic when he finished in the game but emigrated to Australia where he died in September 2003

BILL WHARE – spent his late teenage years and beyond in a Nazi internment camp on his native Guernsey before becoming an ever dependable right back with an effective sliding tackle whose appearances for his only club topped the 300 mark. Like many of his generation, melded into the pub trade when he retired, enjoying a long and fruitful tenancy at the Waggon and Horses in Redhill on the road to Mansfield. Died 1995, aged 71

CHARLIE THOMSON – Chic, as he was affectionately known, had already won a Championship title in 1955 with Chelsea, the London club's first. It was his bravery and agility that were key factors in withstanding Luton's later forays as cramp further reduced the resilience of Forest's ten men. Son of a professional goalkeeper, he began his career at Clyde. Remained in Nottingham but always invited, and accepted, as a guest at reunions for Stamford Bridge old boys. Died in January, aged 78

BOB McKINLAY – legend has become a devalued expression but the Scottish centre half can be described thus in older values when the term actually had some depth of meaning. Arrived at the City Ground as a Scottish junior from Bowhill Rovers and started a club record 682 games for Forest, 265 of those in succession. A gentleman defender, keen gardener and avid pipe smoker, he worked as a prison warden at a young offenders' institute near Lowdham. Died in August 2002, aged 69

JACK BURKITT – 'built like an oak and never knows the meaning of the word 'licked' went the contemporary pen pics for one of the most stylish wing halves of his generation. Oddly that failed to earn him an England cap although the captain was also unerring in distribution and unflappable in the middle of the park. Later as a Forest coach, he taught Henry Newton the basics of solid tackling, instruction that was indelibly imprinted on a generation of 1960s midfield players who presumed, incorrectly, that they were the hardest on the block. Had a brief spell as manager of Notts County before being succeeded by Billy Gray, his inside left in the 1959 Cup Final. Another one club man, Burkitt ran a post office on Oakdale Road in Nottingham before retiring to Sutton-on-Sea. Died September 2003

JEFF WHITEFOOT – joked that he must have been under hypnosis when rejecting Forest as he left Manchester United to join instead Grimsby. Nicknamed 'Sugar' from a contemporary television western character named Tom Brewster in Tenderfoot, he eventually made it from Cleethorpes to Nottingham at the start of the season that yielded the FA Cup. The calling to the bar, public, lounge and tap room, as well as a grocery business, took

the days when posteriors, shins and just about any part of the anatomy was fair game for brutally scavenging centre halves. Scored both goals that beat Cup holders Bolton Wanderers in the quarter finals as well as his header at Wembley. Moved on to Walsall in 1960. Died in 1992

BILLY WALKER (manager) – Forest's second most successful manager, and taking runners-up prize behind Brian Clough is still some tribute. Came to the club shortly before the Second World War and though demoted to the Third Division (South) in 1949, a succession of astute signings saw the club regain their status, culminating in the Final victory ten years later. Walker also won the Cup with Villa as a player, in 1924, and guided Sheffield Wednesday to triumph at Wembley in the 1935 Final. Retired to take up post as honorary committee member in 1960 but dogged by ill-health, he died in 1964, aged 67

BILLY GRAY – his penalty conversion that rescued the tie against Tooting and Mitcham was probably the most decisive moment of Forest's Cup run. He scored four more during that sojourn to Wembley where he turned in a stunning virtuoso at inside left, a position to which Walker converted him after arriving from Burnley as a right winger. Formerly with Leyton Orient and Chelsea, with whom he reached two Cup semi finals, he moved on to Millwall and managed Notts County, for whom he signed Don Masson, before coaching at Fulham. A trained tennis coach, he returned to Nottingham and ran a fish and chip shop and grocery business before taking up duties as a groundsman at the immaculate Raleigh Sports Ground and later the City Ground. He lives in Aspley with his wife Mary

STEWART IMLACH – fleet of foot with a wicked body swerve endemic in impish Scottish wingers, he played possibly the game of his life at Wembley, not only creating the opening goal and tormenting markers but deployed a little deeper to assist McDonald in muting Billy Bingham on Luton's right flank. The subject of a brilliant and poignant book by his son Gary, Imlach's clubs were as wide and varied as his wing play which he coached at clubs such as Notts County and most famously Everton after hanging up his boots. Died October 2001, aged 69

him from the Notts village of East Leake to Oakham in Rutland in which county he now resides

Bottom row from left:
ROY DWIGHT – being an older cousin to Reg Dwight, aka Elton John, is perhaps not something you want to advertise. Another who joined at the start of season, having lost an FA Cup semi final with Fulham the previous April. Apart from his cavalier style and wonderful Final goal, Dwight also scored a hat trick in the second replay that saw Birmingham battered 5-0. Joined the winning parade to the Old Market Square on Monday after leaving hospital with his leg in plaster. Gravesend and Northfleet, Coventry City and Millwall were his later clubs. Ironically returned to Tooting and Mitcham as manager in the 1970s and in charge at Dartford before managing a Crayford greyhound

track in latter years. Died 2002, aged 69

JOHNNY QUIGLEY – richly talented Scot whose eternal gratitude in club folklore was secured when he scored the only goal of the game to beat Aston Villa at Hillsborough. An inventive inside right, he later went on to Huddersfield, Bristol City and Mansfield Town where he encouraged a young but disillusioned Duncan McKenzie, on-loan at the Stags from Forest. A buoyant, well loved and known character in local Notts football. Died December 2004, aged 69

TOMMY WILSON – although born in Bedlington, Northumberland, he was discovered locally playing for pit team Cinderhill. A model of consistency, robust and fearless leader of the line, traits that epitomised most centre forwards in

SAFE HANDS:
Chic Thomson
makes a clean
catch to calm
early nerves as
Bob McKinlay
looks on

Chapter 5

The Empire strikes back

The flying Scotsmen and other heroes

IF it was a triumph in adversity, it was also a triumph of one man's tactical vision. Billy Walker had been an FA Cup winner with Aston Villa in 1924 and guided Sheffield Wednesday to their Wembley victory at the same stage eleven years later.

Without a shadow of a doubt, though, this was his finest hour and a half in his managerial capacity.

It had taken him ten years to revive the club that had fallen from grace

to the Third Division (South), restoring membership among the elite in 1957 with a combination of canny acquisitions from across the football spectrum and indeed the age range. Doug Lishman, from Arsenal, and Eddie Baily, from Tottenham Hotspur's 'push and run' 1951 title-winning team, had been earlier successes that did the job, filled the vacancy and then moved on when surplus to requirements.

Chic Thomson, a Championship winner with Chelsea in 1955, was another veteran to whom Walker turned but there was also Tommy Wilson, a raw right winger for Cinderhill Colliery in the Notts Alliance who Walker signed then nurtured to be a bludgeoning and prolific centre forward.

Similarly he bought Roy Dwight, normally a centre forward, and transformed him into an enterprising right winger laden with goals. Billy Gray arrived from Burnley, where he was Turf Moor's leading scorer in his first season, and persuaded him that inside left was his best position. His partnership with Stewart Imlach, the first Scottish player to be capped while playing for Forest, was a remarkable and enthralling feature of the club's progress to Wembley that season.

In fact it was Imlach's shimmying run and centre in the ninth minute, after Jeff Whitefoot and Gray had instigated the move, that created that

GOTCHA! Above and left, Ron Baynham finally lays hands, this before gloved wonders arrived in multi-coloured jerseys between the sticks, on the ball. A rare touch of the leather orb must have been something of a novelty for the Luton custodian during Forest's blistering opening gambit

ROY OF THE
ROVERS: Roy
Dwight's left foot
makes the perfect
connection with
Stewart Imlach's
centre, above, and
the goalscorer is up
in the air as the ball
fizzes unerringly
into the top corner
of the net. 1-0, nine
minutes gone

memorable first goal and set Forest on such a glorious but torturous path to FA Cup victory.

Dwight, drifting towards the penalty spot, met the pass with a ferocious left-foot shot that remains one of Wembley's cleanest and truest strikes to this day, in its execution and accuracy one to rival one of Bobby Charlton's many specials at the Empire Stadium.

Five minutes later it was 2-0. Jack Burkitt began the move, Imlach

HEAD-ON TOMMY:
Above, Tommy Wilson is out of sight and Forest should have been as the big centre forward powers a diagonal header from Billy Gray's left wing centre for 2-0 after 14 minutes. Ron Baynham in the Luton goal must have been wondering when the next Forest attack would yield a third! Left, and here's how he did it....

carried it on and Gray, again on the left, directed a far post centre that was headed in by the robust Wilson. Luton, in their first FA Cup Final, were outflanked, outmanoeuvred and utterly outplayed. Field Marshal Montgomery, watching in the Royal Box, may well have approved.

"We could have gone on to score six that day," recalled Jeff Whitefoot, Forest's influential right half. Perhaps Whitefoot's premonition might have been correct and there is an abundance of contemporary written material to support his case but in any event, it was not to be. For one compelling reason.

SPOT THE BALL: Heads up as Allan Brown and Chic Thomson look to the heavens for a high ball that eventually floated safely out of play. Bill Whare does not seem too concerned about its trajectory anyway

SAFE! Just about as Ron Baynham, opposite, ushers a Forest effort wide of the mark. Tommy Wilson's expression tells its own story of how close the Reds came to a third

RESCUE RANGER:
Ron Baynham dives
bravely at Tommy
Wilson's feet to deny
the big forward a
second

JUST FADE AWAY:
Roy Dwight's
angled shot drifts
wide as Forest
continue to pepper
Ron Baynham's
goalmouth from all
angles of the pitch

LUTON CAME TOO: The Hatters did have their moments in that opening salvo from Forest, albeit marginal ones. Bob McKinlay wins the aerial battle with Bob Morton as Allan Brown seeks to pounce on the loose ball ahead of Jack Burkitt

TAKING NO PRISONERS: Joe McDonald ends Billy Bingham's hopes of getting to the byline with a sliding tackle

EXTRA COVER: Chic Thomson leaps to deny the bustling Bob Morton once more with Bob McKinlay in attendance and Bill Whare guarding his line and touching wood for a bit of luck perhaps

STRETCHER CASE: Just over half an hour gone and Luton defender Brendan McNally's accidental collision with Roy Dwight ended the flying winger's participation in the game with a fractured shin bone, presenting Luton with unexpected respite and a gilt-edged chance to make a decent fist of a game in which they had hitherto been second best by a country mile. Trainer Tom Graham keeps Dwight company for a while. As he was being carried onto the stretcher, Dwight turned to McNally and told the right back: "It was not your fault at all Brendan. But I hope we win."

And then there were ten

TWELVE minutes before the interval, Luton defender Brendan McNally collided with Dwight and though the challenge was accidental and innocuous, the Forest goalscorer fractured a shin bone and was stretchered off.

The 'Wembley Hoodoo' as it was known then had visited the stadium once more. Four times since 1952, a Cup Final team had been debilitated through injury, a handicap that could not be rectified in the days before substitutes.

It was a dire situation. The lush Wembley turf had welcomed and beckoned Forest whose natural passing game had flourished in its wide open spaces. Now those same inviting swathes of green must have seemed like acres as one by one, players suffered cramp and crippling

pain in an attempt to compensate for Dwight's absence

When David Pacey at last beat Thomson in the 62nd-minute, Forest fans must have feared the worst for the remaining half hour, an anxious and injury-plagued finale for their players. Despite the best efforts of Allan Brown and Billy Bingham, Forest survived. Just.

For the best part of an hour they had defied Luton and their marvellously composed and dignified wing half Jack Burkitt became the first captain to lift the famous old trophy under the burden of playing with 10 men.

UNDER PRESSURE: The sun has got its hat on and so has Chic Thomson by now, struggling to fend off a Luton centre with Allan Brown again in the thick of things. Tommy Wilson is back to help his defence as Bill Whare heads to safety

HEAD FIRST: Chic Thomson demonstrates his fearless nature by diving at the feet of Luton centre forward Bob Morton as the Hatters increase the tempo

PACEY MAKER: Luton left half David Pacey steals in at the far post to plant a left foot effort beyond Chic Thomson despite the presence of Joe McDonald, Jack Burkitt and Bill Whare. That was 62 minutes gone, more importantly 28 remaining and counting. In fact, referee Clough would allow a further four minutes of agonising injury time

"The whole experience, the Cup fun, the Final, was incredible," Whitefoot recalled. "The team played some fantastic football, I mean really fantastic. To feet, all the time, quick and sharp. There was no stopping us on the day. Remember that after the semi final we hardly won a league game [three in 13 in fact, including a 5-1 defeat at Luton Town].

"It was an amazing year, my first for the club. Simply amazing. There was a great camaraderie, not because we socialised together really. We all

went out now and again but others, like Jack Burkitt, kept themselves to themselves.

"But that day at Wembley I believe we might have gone on and broken the Cup Final record. You could sense it the way we were playing. Roy's injury put an end to that. The final whistle was just a blessed relief. We were all absolutely on our knees by then. Totally cream-crackered!"

HANGING IN THERE: Forest were wilting visibly in the sun with the gallant Bob McKinlay, left, grounded and Jeff Whitefoot and Bill Whare toiling to get back and cover. Fortunately Chic Thomson's acrobatics thwarted Allan Brown as Luton pressed relentlessly for a leveller

FA Cup Final: Nottingham Forest v Luton Town, on Saturday, May 2 at Wembley Stadium Nottingham Forest: *Thomson; Whare, McDonald; Whitefoot, McKinlay, Burkitt; Dwight, Quigley, Wilson, Gray, Imlach.* Luton Town: *Baynham; Hawkes, McNally; Pacey, Owen, Goves; Gregory, Cummins, Morton, Brown, Bingham.* Goal-scorers: *For Forest, Dwight (9), Wilson (13). For Luton, Pacey (62)* Result: *Nottingham Forest 2 Luton Town 1* Attendance: *100,000*

QUEEN OF THE MIDLANDS: 'And jolly well played' may have been the gist as HMQ presents the Cup to captain Jack Burkitt. 'And were you amused, ma'am?' is unlikely to have been the retort from one of the Black Country's most stoic sons

IT'S OURS: Below Jack Burkitt has the biggest beam in Wembley Stadium as he turns to accept the plaudits and lift the famous old trophy to the Forest fans, getting a slap on the back from his chairman Harold Alcock and an approving smile from the Duke of Hazard, aka Prince Philip

BREAKING THE HOODOO

WILL you walk into my parlour? said the spider to the fly. Mary Howitt's whimsical poem for children evoked echoes of Wembley Stadium's invitation to FA Cup finalists during the 1950s, tempted by the lure of its rich but clogging surface and the promise of fame and relative fortune within its boundaries. Four times in the previous seven years the losers had been reduced to 10 men with another Final blighted by serious injury.

●*1952: Arsenal Welsh international right back Wally Barnes damages knee ligaments and is carried off as Newcastle United win 1-0 against the 10 men*
●*1953: Wing half Eric Bell tears a hamstring and though he scores a goal as a passenger for Bolton Wanderers, his team finally capitulate under the handicap, losing to Blackpool in the Matthews Final that sees Stan Mortensen score a hat trick in a 4-3 win after being 3-1 down.*
●*1955: Jimmy Meadows, the Manchester City full back, suffers a knee injury and is forced out of the Final which Newcastle United win 3-1 in his absence. Ominous shades of déjà vu as Meadows twists his knee in the same corner as Barnes was injured, trying to tackle the same player, Robert Mitchell*
●*1956: Manchester City goalkeeper Bert Trautmann plays the last quarter of an hour with a fractured neck after diving at the feet of a Birmingham forward. The former German POW remains on the pitch and escapes with a Cup winners' medal in a 3-1 win.*
●*1957: Another year, another goalkeeper, this time Manchester United's Roy Wood is clattered by Aston Villa's Peter McParland. The Irishman is technically* within his rights but many feel his premeditated run and body charge that fells Wood and leaves him with a fractured cheek bone is nothing less than cowardly intimidation. With Jackie Blanchflower in goal, United, the red hot favourites and League champions, lose 2-1, McParland scoring both of the goals. It was to be a last Wembley Final for Duncan Edwards and several of the Busby Babes who died at Munich in February the following year.

And later....
●*1960: Blackburn Rovers left back Dave Whelan, he of the JJB Sports Empire, fractures a leg as his team are drubbed 3-0 by Wolverhampton Wanderers in one of Wembley's dullest finales*
●*1961: Right back Len Chalmers, of Leicester City, is left hobbling with an ankle injury for most of the game as Tottenham Hotspur claim the vaunted Double in a 2-0 win*
●*1965: Liverpool's Gerry Byrne becomes the latest casualty with a fractured collar bone sustained in the third minute of the game with Leeds United. Like most of the viewing public, he endures the remainder of the game in agony, including extra time, before Liverpool secure a first FA Cup 2-1*
●*July 3, 1965: Never let it be said that you could accuse the FA of allowing the winds of change to pass them by. Thirteen years, and more in fact, after it became abundantly clear that an injury depleted side suffered an unfair handicap in not only a showcase final but every Saturday afternoon throughout the season, the ruling body decided to do something about it. Step forward the substitute, singularly correct in its inception, ridiculously superfluous now that television and its moguls have taken over the asylum.*

OUR NAME WAS ON IT ALL ALONG: Far left, the skipper is mobbed by supporters descending from the Royal Box with Billy Gray following closely behind. Stewart Imlach, donning the Cup's lid, is shorn of his front false teeth that regularly came out before games

MONTY'S FIELD DAY: Field Marshal Montgomery discusses tactics in a post-match de-briefing

LAP OF HONOUR: From left, Tommy Wilson, Johnny Quigley, Stewart Imlach, still hanging on to the lid, and Jack Burkitt, still clinging on to the Cup, take a bow before Reds fans. It was the first time a winning Wembley Cup Final team had embarked on a celebration lap of honour, a custom like the pre-match pennant exchange, that mirrored the Continental way of doing things

HAPPY PEOPLE: Tommy Wilson and Jeff Whitefoot hold Jack Burkitt and the FA Cup aloft flanked by Stewart Imlach, with lid, and Billy Gray, on base, alongside trainer Tom Graham

PRIDE OF THE CITY: Was there ever a prouder captain at Wembley on FA Cup Final day?

QUITE REMARKABLE: David Coleman asks the questions for the BBC cameras. Manager Billy Walker is far right

THE CUP THAT CHEERS: Joe McDonald quaffs from a Cup full of champagne, doubtless sinking a few bubbles, in the winners' dressing room

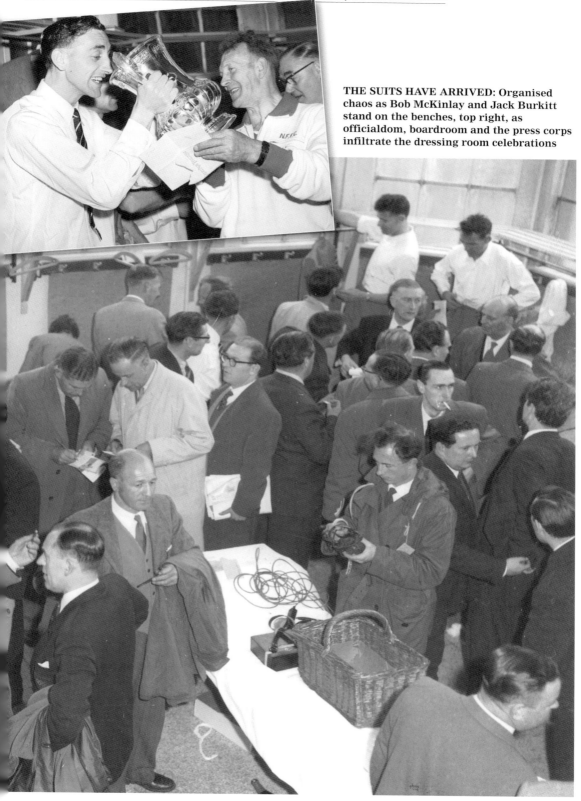

THE SUITS HAVE ARRIVED: Organised chaos as Bob McKinlay and Jack Burkitt stand on the benches, top right, as officialdom, boardroom and the press corps infiltrate the dressing room celebrations

WHAT THE PAPERS SAID: The Football Post and Football News pink 'un celebrate the local heroes....the Toronto Telegram confirms that good news travels fast even if it is 'Notts' Forest! On Monday, The Times reflects the dramatic events of the weekend as only The Times could back then

FOOTBALL POST

Vol. L. No. 37.   SATURDAY, MAY 2, 1959   THREEPENCE

FOREST CUP FINAL SOUVENIR

FOREST WIN THE C

TODAY'S TROPHY   Dwight & Wilson score   THE

AFTER 61 YEARS, FOREST HAVE AGAIN GOT THE FAMOUS CUP IN THEIR POSSESSION. AS EXPECTED, THEY WERE TOO SMART FOR THEIR LUTON OPPONENTS AND WON 2—1.

There was a crowd of 100,000, the receipts totalling £49,708. The teams were introduced to the Duke of Edinburgh and the Duke of Gloucester, president of the FA, Luton first, and when it came to the Reds' turn, the ... Burkitt, after a chat with Jack Burkitt, spent a moment with ... Channel Islander to play in a Final.

RESULT:

Nottm. Forest - 2

NOTTINGHAM FOREST FOOTBALL CLUB

N.F.F.C.

CELEBRATION DINNER

2nd MAY, 1959

H. W. ALCOCK, ESQ.
(Chairman of Nottingham Forest F.C.)
IN THE CHAIR

SAVOY HOTEL   LONDON

CIGARS ALL ROUND: Tom Graham enjoys a Havana in discussion with Harold Alcock while left back Joe McDonald relaxes with a smoke and coffee at the celebration dinner at the Savoy that evening

FOOTBALL NEWS

No. 2,652　　SATURDAY, MAY 2, 1959　　THREEPENCE

OUTFITS FOR
CLIMBING
HIKING
CYCLING
MOTOR-CYCLING
TENTS and CAMP EQUIPMENT
ARMY & GENERAL STORES
NEAR MIDLAND STATION
CARRINGTON ST., NOTTINGHAM

BRIAN
LUDLOW
Phone
NOTTM. 48261
The Midlands Premier
TURF ACCOUNTANT
Head Office LUDLOW HOUSE
DERBY RD., NOTTM.

IT'S FOREST'S CUP

Pacey Scores As Hatters Stage Big Fight-back

INJURIES HIT REDS
AFTER TWO GOALS

TWO golden goals, the first by right winger Roy Dwight after only nine minutes and another five minutes later from Tommy Wilson, had Forest fans cheering themselves hoarse. What a wonderful start !

Then that wretched Wembley hoodoo struck again ! Its victim was Dwight, who was taken to hospital with a suspected fracture of the leg. Brendan McNally, the Luton right back, had cut sho___ a sliding tackle.

The big interval ____
Forest ha___

WEEKEND TELY 10¢

AN EDITION OF

TV Weekly | Weekend MAGAZINE | 16 PAGES COMICS

THE TELEGRAM

TORONTO, SATURDAY, MAY 2, 1959

★ 3 ★　140 PAGES

The Pink Tely
Night
Late Sports

SUNDAY
Sunny, Warm
Low 50
High 75
Details Page Two | COMING UP | 84TH YEAR

Man Short But Takes U-K Cup Final

NOTTS FOREST WINS

Chapter I　...In The Life Of Zura | 2-1 Victory | **Ballet Beats Pucksters And Hipsters**

THE　TIMES　M_

Sporting News (Also on page 4)

TEN MEN CLING TO FRUITS
OF INSPIRED FOOTBALL

FOREST GAIN F.A. CUP AGAINST
LESS GIFTED TEAM

From Our Association Football Correspondent

Nottingham Forest 2, Luton Town 1

A journey that almost took a first step towards disaster down Sandy Lane, Mitcham, some four months ago ended in triumph at Wembley on Saturday when Burkitt led his Nottingham Forest team—what remained of them—up the steps of the royal box to receive the F.A. Cup from the Queen.

Luton Town, sadly but justly, were left behind with heads bowed, knowing in their hearts that they had lacked the stature and

Way—a school marching to call-over. Soon, too, the midland battle hymn of Robin Hood surged on the wind as the first arrow found its mark.

After only 10 minutes Imlach left McNally standing with a flick and acceleration down the left; his diagonal pass from the by-line sped into Dwight's stride as the right wing came through the middle. Baynham never saw the left-footed shot that hit the top corner of his net. It was a glorious goal. Almost at once, by the quarter-hour, Nottingham were two up

Dwight, the Nottingham Forest player (extreme l___

CLEAN SWEEP IN
DAVIS CUP

MILLS LOSES TWO
____ ____ _____

PA___

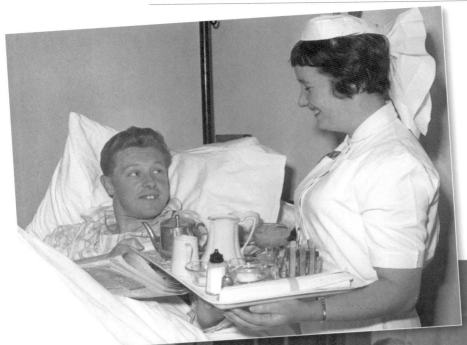

BREAKFAST IN BED: Roy Dwight gets the tea and toast treatment but no silver tray

ANGELS AT HIS SHOULDER: His leg in plaster, Roy Dwight gets a helping hand from nurses as he leaves Wembley Hospital for the return trip to Nottingham on Monday morning

Chapter 6

First class return

The Cup came too

SUNDAY. A day of rest, of calm relaxation. A day of quiet deliberation. In the days before Sainsbury's set about infiltrating the sanctity of the Sabbath and retail therapy replaced religious instruction, the players of Nottingham Forest had ample spare time and solitude to reflect on the historic events of the previous day.

The entourage had retreated to the Sussex coast and Hove after the Saturday night banquet at the Savoy Hotel. Lunching at a seafront restaurant, they told the manageress Doris Woods that they'd like to see an edited recording of the televised game.

Given the mind-numbingly blanket and increasingly inane coverage of football today, it is difficult to image players not being able to see themselves randomly on the small screen but of course it was a novelty back in 1959 with the FA Cup Final the only guarantee of an appearance in their chosen vocation on the magic box.

HELLO AGAIN: Roy Dwight, with his dedicated nurse who had brought him breakfast earlier in the day, is reunited with his captain Jack Burkitt and the FA Cup at St Pancras. The players had presented him with his medal on a Saturday night visit to Wembley Hospital after the Final tie

Obligingly, Mrs Woods invited them all back to her flat to watch the highlights that afternoon. And what thoughts must have been flashing through their minds as they sat and stared at the television.

By then captain Jack Burkitt's arm was in a sling, an injury he had braved from early on, thinking at first it was dislocated. How would Forest have coped with nine men? Mission impossible certainly.

And then there was Billy Gray, who almost didn't start, instead a pre-match injection in an injured foot was the best kept secret of the day. As he watched himself carry the ebony plinth of the Cup around the field in celebration, his relief that the gamble had paid off was probably only eclipsed by that of his manager Billy Walker.

There had been other angst-ridden moments that went unnoticed to the causal spectator, too. A fierce shot that dazed Joe McDonald, the tenacious Scottish full back who barely allowed the dangerous Billy Bingham a kick on the day. His former Sunderland team mate had scored six goals in the competition that season including the solitary one that sunk Third Division Norwich City in the semi final replay but he scarcely caught a glimpse of the white posts in the shadows of Wembley's Twin Towers as McDonald and Stewart Imlach, deployed a little deeper as the nature of the game altered, maintained an iron grip on the Northern Ireland international.

For Chic Thomson, the split second when Allan Brown's header rebounded off his post when the goalkeeper was for once beaten most likely inspired a few retrospective palpitations. "It was my one worrying moment," he later said, although he might have known his goal was secure considering the lucky mascot, or mascots, he was humping around with him. A chain of medals he took, by accident, to the first game at Tooting and Mitcham. "I've had them with me ever since."

The magnificent six were: First Division title medal, Football Combination winners (Chelsea), Scottish B League Championship title, Scottish

Continued on page 114

PLATFORM FOR SUCCESS: The thin controller, aka the stationmaster at St Pancras, escorts the Forest players and the silverware to the Nottingham train

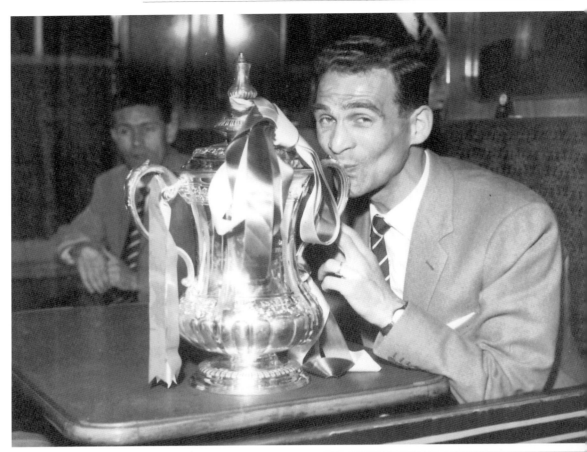

HOMEWARD BOUND: A pot to cherish for the captain with Joe McDonald in the background

ACES HIGH: Solo was a favourite card game for Jack Burkitt, seen here playing with a Forest committee member and the FA Cup

FIRST THE CUP, NOW THE SAUCERS: That's British Rail for you! Steward, sorry Stewart Imlach balances the coffees and biscuits as he jinks down the corridor while smoking a cigar. As easy as opening up the Luton right flank no doubt

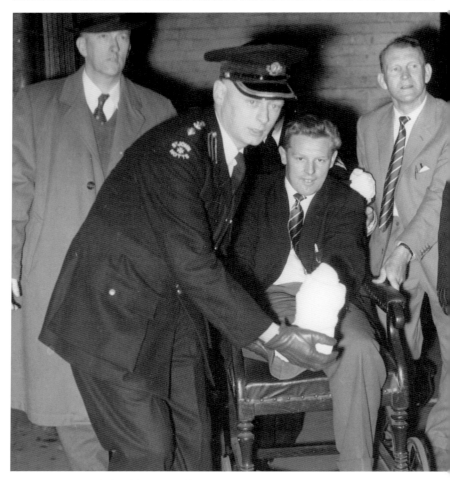

LEG UP: Trainer Tom Graham, who had anxiously escorted Roy Dwight from the pitch alongside the stretcher bearers of the St John Ambulance Brigade, is once again by the stricken player's side as he makes his way from the Midland Station platform to street level

League Cup and the Glasgow Charity Cup Competition (Clyde) and Army Championship winners' medal (REME).

A first team to lift the trophy with ten men, a first Channel Islander to win a Cup Final medal in Bill Whare.

Yet after David Pacey's goal, the remaining 28 minutes must have passed as slowly as a Latin revision class without the bewildered boredom factor as Reds fans rooted for the final whistle.

But Mr Clough did Forest no favours. In an act of time-keeping that tips some modern managers close to the edge of spontaneous combustion, Jack Clough added a further four minutes on to compensate for the assorted injuries, Roy Dwight's delayed departure from the pitch being the main hindrance as well as several Forest players suffering from cramp in the latter stages.

The nervous exhaustion was strictly confined to the people in red on the terraces.

And so on to Monday, to the Dwight reunion and the short and sweet journey home...

SEEING IS BELIEVING: Young schoolboys get a close-up glimpse of the trophy as the less than thin controller, aka the Midland's stationmaster, guides the captain and his team out of the Station

DYNAMIC DUO: Or maybe that should be holy trinity, for while Jack Burkitt and Billy Walker make a fitting and inspirational pair, the FA Cup adds up to a triangle that is eternal in the eyes of Forest fans

THE THIN BLUE LINE: Is it a bird? Is it a plane? Neither, nor superman. Just a team of dogged First Division footballers earning around £20 a week who lifted themselves to a higher level for one captivating season and one final, marvellous effort. Shades of Beatlemania to come indicate the level of adulation they enjoyed during that long hot summer of 1959 as the crowds jostle for position outside Midland Station

Last leg by bus

O N the morning after the night before, the Guardian Journal had the tally at 70,000. The Evening Post revised it for their later editions to 200,000. Just how many people actually lined the triumphant route to celebrate Forest's Cup victory from the moment they left Midland Station at 6.40pm and then witnessed its finale in the Old Market Square on that Monday May 4 is uncertain.

But to judge by the photographs, there were an awful lot. And a few more besides.

From the station, down along Queen's Drive, across Kirkewhite Street

THE COACH NOW LEAVING PLATFORM 10: The Robin Hood bus with its motorcycle escort weaves its way out of Midland Station and down Queen's Drive. Over the page, Jack Burkitt answers the fans' call to show them the Cup as the players sit astride the openings at the top of the specially adapted coach

and up London Road through Carlton Road, the Robin Hood bus crawled at walking pace, everywhere and everyone ablaze with red and white banners, scarves, hats, coats and umbrellas on the balmiest of May nights, all resplendent in the colour theme of the hour.

Hawkers, or street barrow boys, had one of their better days and nights, able to sell anything for cash as long it came in red and white and as long as they were within touching distance of the seven mile route.

Alfred Street, Mansfield Road, Gregory and Lenton Boulevards by the Forest Recreation ground and Goose Fair site, down Derby Road and beyond Chapel Bar where several young folk fainted, a few of the 50 estimated people who suffered from giddiness amid the sudden claustrophobia created

LONDON ROAD: The Nottingham Canal runs adjacent to the route as the Forest coach passes by neighbouring Meadow Lane

by unprecedented numbers in the city centre and its environs.

Not even a royal visit could hold a torch to the clamour of folk desperate to catch sight of the FA Cup winners, particularly the cheeky little chappie that was Roy Dwight, pushed along by St John Ambulance men and police escorts in his wheelchair that brought up the rear of the party as it ambled along the Processional Way from the north west corner of 'Slab' Square.

A red sea of sorts was parted down the middle as some of the extra 200 police officers on duty that night corralled a noisy but jovial crowd that could have been anything up to 70,000 strong as it swarmed about the square and obliterated from view its surrounding arterial roads.

"We want Roy," they chanted but the fans were told by the Lord Mayor that they could not have him. In fact Alderman Joseph Littlefair's speech was swamped by the cacophony and uproarious nature of the huge crowd, many of whom had gathered earlier in the day even before the

FOUR-LEGGED FRIENDS: Mounted police were also on patrol to keep a delirious audience in line as scenes like these were repeated all over the city. Above, the coach ascends Alfred Street

Forest squad had left London's St Pancras.

A pause for thought for the defeated Luton Town team, sporting to a man, and then as red and white balloons plummeted from the Council House balcony above, Jack Burkitt responded to the Lord Mayor's valiant but futile address.

"I read in one paper that it was the most glorious Final since the end of the war, or for many years," the captain bellowed into the BBC microphone. "If that is so, all I can say is that the reception which you are giving us tonight is one of the most glorious for a Cup Final team."

And with that the biggest cheer of the evening and the players were gone inside, one final appearance on the balcony before the party festivities began.

TRANSPORT OF DELIGHT:
Left, the City Transport offices are coming up on the left of Lower Parliament Street with the Boots Island industries dominating the skyline in the background.
Above, recognise anyone?

SQUARE BASHING ON PARADE: The Old Market Square had never seen anything like it. Estimates varied between 30,000-70,000 turned out on Monday evening beneath the gaze of Griffin and Spalding, H Samuel the jewellers and the city hub's other familiar stores around the quadrangle. In the very middle, the Forest team, with Roy Dwight lagging behind in a wheelchair, made their dramatic entrance to the Council House building

STANDING ROOM ONLY: The trolleybuses had no hope of running on time, or running at all as local folk lingered long into the night

LEADERS OF THE PACK: Jack Burkitt and Billy Walker lead from the front. How else?

CHAIN GANG: Jack Burkitt and Roy Dwight have the Cup and the Lord Mayor has his own medal to show off at the entrance doors of the Council House

Painting the town red

ONCE inside, Roy Dwight continued to be the focus of attention. In fact, earlier in the day he had been making a fuss over others, and a presentation of his own, when the winger handed over an iced cake in the shape of Wembley Stadium to the staff and nurses who had looked after him at Wembley Hospital following his premature departure from the Cup Final.

Again there were more speeches and conviviality at the official reception hosted by the chairman Harold Alcock and his wife Margaret.

"I only hope I shall live to see Nottingham Forest champions of Division One," said long-serving secretary Noel Watson while Alderman Fred Mitchell, one of the city fathers, recalled the triumphant scenes when Forest last returned with the FA Cup, in May 1898.

"I can vividly recall the grand parade when the club's headquarters were in Maypole Yard," he told the 300 guests of City Council and

PLAYTIME ANTICS: Schoolchildren shake a leg and a rattle beneath their banners awaiting the team's arrival for the Civic reception

Continued on page 134

THE LIONS' TALE:
The entrance steps
between the stone
lions of the Council
House are festooned
with balloons as
the Lord Mayor,
Alderman Joseph
Littlefair, feels
obliged to make a
speech to the masses

IT'S THAT MAN
AGAIN:
No, not the captive
audience that is
Roy Dwight but
Alderman Littlefair
introducing himself
to the injured winger
with his fractured
shin in a plaster cast

Corporation officials and nearly 100 Forest club members at the reception.

Fittingly, though, it was Jack Burkitt who caught the mood of the moment and what most of the Forest squad were thinking.

"It [the bus journey around the city] was something I shall never forget, I am sure. I was more nervous in Nottingham tonight than I ever felt at Wembley Stadium – before we started our great struggle."

From the banqueting hall to the dance floor was the next step when many of the Forest players decamped to the Sherwood Rooms, except Dwight.

He was whisked away by ambulance to the General Hospital for overnight rest in readiness for an examination by a club specialist the following day.

Stewart Imlach and Jeff Whitefoot arrived by taxi as 50 or so late night revellers awaited their arrival, seeking autographs and wanting to wish them well.

LAST LINE OF DEFENCE: Chic Thompson and his wife Pat are greeted by Harold and Margaret Alcock

HAMMER BLOW: Jimmy Barrett arrives with his wife. Barrett was a prolific scorer after his move from West Ham United with 30 goals during the 1957 Second Division promotion winning season and though one of three reserves for the Final, he had been reduced to the first team fringes after sustaining badly torn ligaments in December that same promotion year

It was as the pair were piloted through the crowds by doormen that the crowd burst out laughing at the sight of an Alsatian dressed in a red shirt and white shorts.

His owner told onlookers that the dog went by the name of Rex.... an apposite finale to an astonishing, undulating and absorbing journey that had begun in Morden, Surrey, several months earlier.

For a few days at least, Imlach, Whitefoot and the Forest XI of 1959 were indeed kings among men. And feted accordingly by their loyal subjects.

SEMI ATTACHED:
Johnny Quigley, who
scored the precious
semi final goal,
accompanied by his
wife

CAPTAIN'S KISS: The Cup and the captain are still not parted as he and his wife Hazel share a tender moment at the official banquet. Johnny Quigley, and Tom Graham keep a vigil with Tommy Wilson squeezing into the photograph, second right

NAP HAND: Billy Gray, who scored five goals en route to Wembley including the vital but controversial equalising penalty against Tooting, enters the Council House with his wife Mary

WINGED WONDER: Margaret Alcock shakes hands with Stewart Imlach while the chairman greets his wife Joan, partially hidden by the Scottish winger

OLD HAND: Bill Morley, a stalwart of the 1957 campaign that restored First Division status, is welcomed

LADY IN RED? No-one is quite sure who the two gentleman at this table, top right, are but could it be that Gina Lollobrigida popped over from Italy to provide even more glamour to the occasion?

LOYALTY BONUS: Veteran Jack Hutchinson and his wife share the limelight, right. The full back, born in Codnor, joined the club during the Second World War and was another regular during the 1957 promotion push. He played his last game for the club, his 254th, in September 1958

YOU LUCKY PEOPLE! Tommy Trinder's famous catchphrase might have applied to Forest's early escapades at Tooting and Mitcham. The comedian and Fulham chairman was a guest of honour in Nottingham after he and singer Alma Cogan had entertained the squad at the Savoy banquet on Saturday night

FIRST RESERVE: Opposite page, top, Geoff Thomas, the 12th man at Wembley, and Bill Morley with their wives

HARD CASE: Football League secretary Alan Hardaker (far left) was among the guests. When he introduced the League Cup the following year, he said the FA Cup was the Ascot of football compared to the league's own competition, with he described as Derby Day at Epsom

KING OF SPIN: Former Notts cricketer Ken Smales and partner, left. A shoulder injury the previous year ended Smales' career at Trent Bridge, a new and enduring one beginning at the City Ground the same summer. He succeeded Noel Watson as secretary in 1961 and served the club over several decades that included the glorious Clough era

SPORTS REPORT: The Evening Post's Harry Richards, right, who reported on the game and later became respected Sports Editor at the newspaper, and his wife

FRIENDS OF THE MIRTH: Below: and over the page, Stewart Imlach and his wife Joan and friends

FOUR OF A KIND: Young Scottish forward Chris Joyce, who crossed the Trent to join Notts County that summer, John Armstrong, Calvin Palmer and Ken Simcoe

CROSS SECTION: Opposite and the following five pages, members of the City constabulary, entrepreneurs and friends and relatives of the high and mighty and the not so high and mighty were among the party guests who enjoyed the company of the Forest players

THANKS FOR THE MEMORY: Albert Stapleton, the Forest man for the Nottingham Evening News, echoes the thoughts and feelings of thousands of local folk when he expresses gratitude to the club chairman for allowing him to share the experience of a lifetime

London Office
THE NEWSPAPER HOUSE
8-16 GREAT NEW STREET, E.C.4.
Telephone
FLEET STREET 1030

Telephone
NOTTINGHAM 45911 (20 LINES)
Telegrams
"EVENING NEWS
NOTTINGHAM"

The Nottingham Evening News Ltd.

Branch Offices
MANSFIELD, 48 White Hart Street — Tel 96
GRANTHAM, 19 London Road — Tel. 249 & 1012
BOSTON, Sibsey Lane — Tel. 3876
SPALDING, 1 Double Street — Tel 2058
NEWARK, 28 Market Place — Tel. 2342
SUTTON-IN-ASHFIELD, 25 Slater St. — Tel. 2406

Head Office:

PARLIAMENT STREET.

NOTTINGHAM

May 5, 1959

H.W.Alcock Esq,

Dear Mr.Alcock,

May I take this opportunity of expressing on behalf of my wife and myself, our very sincere thanks for allowing us to witness your magnificient and most memorable Wembley triumph and for the privilege at being present at your most wonderful banquet.

Many thanks to you and your committee and indeed to everybody connected with your magnificient club.

If ever team spirit was in evidence, it was on Saturday, with such splendid organisation and I wish you every success for the future.

Yours sincerely,

Albert E Stapleton

DRIVEN BY SUCCESS: As reward for their Cup exploits, the club received sponsored cars from Oscroft's of Castle Boulevard, the Vauxhall Victor De-Luxe. From left to right: Chic Thomson, Johnny Quigley, G Smalley, committee, Harold Alcock, club chairman, Jack Burkitt, Bob McKinlay, Stewart Imlach, Bill Whare, Billy Walker, manager, and Frank Sisson, committee. How little did some of the players know that it was nearly the end of the road for their time in Nottingham?